Genghis Khan

The Ancient Secrets and Strategies of Genghis Khan

(Genghis Khan Uniter of the Tribes and Conqueror of the World)

William Jones

Published By **Bengion Cosalas**

William Jones

All Rights Reserved

Genghis Khan: The Ancient Secrets and Strategies of Genghis Khan (Genghis Khan Uniter of the Tribes and Conqueror of the World)

ISBN 978-1-77485-535-5

No part of this guidebook shall be reproduced in any form without permission in writing from the publisher except in the case of brief quotations embodied in critical articles or reviews.

Legal & Disclaimer

The information contained in this ebook is not designed to replace or take the place of any form of medicine or professional medical advice. The information in this ebook has been provided for educational & entertainment purposes only.

The information contained in this book has been compiled from sources deemed reliable, and it is accurate to the best of the Author's knowledge; however, the Author cannot guarantee its accuracy and validity and cannot be held liable for any errors or omissions. Changes are periodically made to this book. You must consult your doctor or get professional medical advice before using any of the suggested remedies, techniques, or information in this book.

Upon using the information contained in this book, you agree to hold harmless the Author from and against any damages, costs, and expenses, including any legal fees potentially resulting from the application of any of the information provided by this guide. This disclaimer applies to any damages or injury caused by the use and application, whether directly or indirectly, of any advice or information presented, whether for breach of contract, tort, negligence, personal injury, criminal intent, or under any other cause of action.

You agree to accept all risks of using the information presented inside this book. You need to consult a professional medical practitioner in order to ensure you are both able and healthy enough to participate in this program.

TABLE OF CONTENTS

Introduction 1

Chapter 1: Setting The Stage - A Historical Timeline 4

Chapter 2: Genghis Khan's Early Life And Family 10

Chapter 3: The Bekhter's Death And The Backlash 22

Chapter 4: Genghis Khan's Rise To Power 28

Chapter 5: The Yassa 91

Chapter 6: The Defeat Of The Tatars 100

Chapter 7: Jurkin Betrayal And Khan's Message 107

Chapter 8: Tatar Defeated Twice 118

Chapter 9: The Naiman Confederacy 129

Chapter 10: Re Conquering The World- Western Xia 134

Chapter 11: Jin And His Legacy 143

Chapter 12: Genghis' Various Sexual Relationships With Kids 147

Chapter 13: The Way He Unified Mongolian Federations 158

Chapter 14: His Military Projects 167

Conclusion 183

Introduction

What are the things you'll remember from your classes in history? You might remember a short discussion about world leaders who were controlled through the sheer power of evil. You may prefer to remember the fictional tales that were written, or even turned into a film or TV show. The details and historical stories of the same man are usually bloody, with the intention of demonstrating the evil a ruler can be, while also providing an awe-inspiring feeling. The man in question, the legend --is Genghis Khan. Genghis Khan is not an imaginary character that was blocked by China and the Chinese, but real-life person who defeated the entirety of China and expanded into the west prior to his death.

Genghis Khan is fascinating due to his ability to ascend from a disregarded leader to become the most powerful leader of his time. His innateness and ambitions have brought the world advancements that we've never seen before. Within 25 years, and with the founding of the Mongol Empire, Genghis Khan defeated more than the Romans could achieve in just four years (Weatehrford 2004).

Genghis Khan was an ace of battle of incredible power, intelligence, as well as a name that brought the fear of all those who were against Genghis Khan. Genghis Khan is one of the men with a lasting legacy to his grandchildren and children which is still discussed with amazement and awe.

Investigating the real story of a leader who was so powerful allows you to understand that even from the smallest "ashes" in the world it is possible to climb, survive and even lead. Genghis Khan's life wasn't one of weakness and palaces. It was a series of challenges which drove the Khan to be successful. Genghis Khan was able to make himself legendary, and even immortalized in the history books because of his incredible skills. Genghis Khan built an army that was so powerful that his enemies fell in defeat. He achieved this by requiring the loyalty of his followers and forming the elite troops of 100,000 soldiers. Of course, he had fewer soldiers than his opposition, but more powerful and more mobile.

Can we really call the leader of this group to be a villain? Did he really stand up for his people when faced with opposition? The scholars debate these questions and will debate them for centuries to come since without living through the same period, it is hard to fully comprehend the motivations of the leader that are buried in mythology.

The book that does not discuss which Genghis Khan is a heroic figure, or a villain. The book will take a look through his death and life victories and the legacy of his life to provide readers with entertainment, information and a new debate.

What would Genghis Khan have made it through his life, overcoming all obstacles his enemies, had he not have to endure the utter humiliation of abandonment? Every person has a unique background and it's the challenges we face that could or might not strengthen us. Is Genghis Khan's life in the beginning the reason why he pushed himself to the outskirts of Mongolia to establish laws and rules that benefitted all those who remained loyal to Genghis Khan?

Explore the debate and find the most likely responses. In those responses you can determine which character was hero or an evil person.

Chapter 1: Setting The Stage - A Historical Timeline

Genghis Khan's and east rule are just a fraction of what was going on in the world of the time. Sure, he was capable of expanding his empire and control China and became a warlord of repute but he also faced the ire of many countries. If you don't understand what "stage" his battles took place on, you'll not be able comprehend his feats of strength.

Mongolia

Presently, Mongolia is a sovereign state with no landlocked borders located in East Asia. In Genghis Khan's time, it expanded to encompass China and areas of Russia and even threatened some countries in the west. Mongolia was the home of various nomadic kingdoms which included Genghis Khan's empire that established the Yuan Dynasty. Xiongnu, Xianbei, Turkic Khaganate along with the Rouran are just a few the largest empires.

The Xiongnu Empire was formed in 209 BCE. It was the time when Xiongnu beat the Yuezhi and took over their "steppes" in central and east Asia. In the early days, Mongolia was only slightly bigger than modern-day Mongolia.

Genghis Khan's birth occurred in 1162, but certain scholars dispute the date. It wasn't until 1206 when Genghis Khan's empire was established. Mongol Empire, ruled by Genghis Khan and his famed grandson Kublai Khan, was formed.

In 1260 in 1260, the Mongol Empire was split into the four lesser empires. It was named after the Yuan Dynasty ruled in China and they were the Golden Hordes located in Russia as well as the Chaghatai in Central Asia, and the Ilkhanate which was ruled by Persia. The majority of the four empires could survive until into the fourteenth century. The only exception was the Chaghatai Dynasty who lasted up to 1658.

The Yuan Dynasty started by Kublai Khan was ended in 1368. The Emperor Toghon Temur was pushed out of China by to the Mongols back to their smaller border. However, it wasn't all that was left of Genghis Khan's legacy. Genghis Khan's successors remained and ruled in Mongolia and some in kingdoms across Asia including his final ruling family member. Alim Khan was the emir of Bukhara from 1920 to 1920. He was the ruler of Uzbekistan (Weatherford 2004, 2004).

China's Story

The first Chinese dynasty began around 2070 BCE. At the time of 221, BCE, China had the First Unification of Imperial China in the Qin Dynasty. It was the time when Qin Dynasty ended in 207 BCE. In 207 BCE, China's Qin Dynasty was surrendered over to Liu Bang and the founder of the Han Dynasty.

The Han Dynasty Ruled until 220 AD. In the year 220 AD, Cao Pi was Chancellor and ruler, and was replacing the Emperor Xian. Cao Pi called China, Cao Wei.

The Middle Dynasties were next, that lasted until the mid-point in the ninth century. In the 9th century, Five Dynasties and Ten Kingdoms reigned from 907 until 960. In the year 960, General Zhao Kuangyin took on the Chinese emperor and initiated his own Song Dynasty.

It was that Song Dynasty that was in control in Genghis Khan's time. Based on the various sources you have read, Kublai Khan started the Yuan Dynasty in 1271, and the Song Dynasty was completely ended in 1279. Kublai Khan ruled his empire in Dadu which is today

Beijing till his passing. It was the Ming Dynasty followed the Mongols leaving China which began in 1368. It ended in 1644. This was when they became the Qing Dynasty started its rule that lasted until 1911.

Russia

Russian customs state that Viking Rurik was the first Viking to arrive in Russia and established the Novgorod Dynasty in the year 862. The majority of Russia was situated by the west side of the expanse, but there were certain Russian territories making their way to east during the eleventh century. The great dukes of Kiev had a central power, which allowed Russia to be protected however, this did not prevent Russia from wanting to expand its territories or its Khans from protecting the territory until he was able to demolish Kiev and divide the territory. There was a time when tribute collectors worked for the Mongols. The dukes used them to control their power as well as a trade centers in Moscow.

Korea

Korea specifically, and the area that is currently North Korea, bordered Russia and

China. Through the Mongol expansion, the region that is now Korea was also regarded as an area that could be conquered. Korea was divided into Three Kingdoms, which became unification by Silla to form a single political power. The event occurred around 935 AD. Goryeo was the ruler of that year, bringing to an end Silla and the Three Kingdoms and Silla. Korea was always in conflict and trade with China as early as the thirteenth century. It was also in the 13th century that it was the time that Mongol Empire invaded weak Goryeo in order to force it to become a vassalage location up to the point that the Yuan dynasty fell and General Yi Seong-gye became capable of establishing the capital city Joseon in 1388.

Eurasia

Around 1000 AD, in the Roman Empire also known as the Byzantine Empire by that time and the Ghaznavid Empire of Iran, Chola Dynasty in India and the Fatimid Caliphate from Egypt were in the ascendancy. Western Europe and several other regions were not as technologically advanced and had lower populations. Genghis Khan did manage to reach Western Europe, but he did not want to keep their land, as per Weatehrford the creator of Genghis Kahn and the Making of the Modern World. Instead, his adventures within China, India, Russia and the region that is now known as the Middle East held more technology and knowledge than Europe. Instead of grabbing the land of Western Europe it was a place he left with the knowledge gained.

He did make his way toward Central Asia trying to control the Aral Sea and Yellow Sea of China. Kublai Khan worked his way further to Volga and then gaining control over his Black Sea, and ensuring that the Mongol Empire grew to extreme power.

Genghis Khan seized Belarus and Hungary and threatened the his control over Poland and Romania following his defeat of Nan Chung, China.

In this time-line, you'll be able to begin making sense of the growth of the Mongol Empire, and how the power Genghis Khan accumulated within such a short time.

Chapter 2: Genghis Khan's Early Life And Family

Genghis Khan is translated to "universal ruler" in English. Genghis Khan was a fitting name to replace his name, Temujin. The beginning of the life of Temujin is a source of confusion and myth. Every historical writer has their personal view about his life, what is true and what is a myth. A ruler who relied on fear to accomplish amazing feats, may have boosted his fame by changing some of his own tale.

John Weatherford, a professor of anthropology, carried out a lengthy study of Genghis Khan's life and death and his conquers. He believes that Temujin was raised in a dangerous environment, where enslavement, murder and kidnapping were commonplace.

There is consensus among historians that Temujin was a son of an exile. The evidence from the past suggests the idea that he was buried in the grasslands of temperate climate or in the steppes that surrounded Mongolia to pass away. It is believed that he likely only interacted with a handful of people in his early years. He didn't get any formal training, but what he did receive was enough to be a successful global leader.

At an early age, Temujin knew of, in horrendous detail, the human range of emotions (Weatherford 2004). He soon discovered what it meant be awed, to desire and to be a victim and be cruel to others.

Temujin's father's, as per Rusty Szmanski's findings was a chieftain of his clan, the Royal Bojigh family, which was part of the Mongols. The research suggests that at the age of 10 old Temujin's father passed away because of greed or other emotions. The father died of poisoning by the rivals (Martin,). At the time , tribal law did not have a specific procedure for succession of the newly elected regent. Temujin was chosen to be the regent however, his tribe did not abide by this rule. Instead of staying with Temujin they departed from Temujin.

Certain scholars would want you to think that the man was by himself. They want you to believe that he was left to make do with what he had. They want you to believe that he was digging up roots and owned seven sheep. The cattle and sheep were money to the Mongols

So the fact that he was left with just two sheep would suggest that Temujin was poor according to Mongol norms.

John Weatherford's research suggests that Genghis Khan was the one who killed his elder brother. He also claims that Temujin was kidnapped and forced to enslaved by a opposing clan. made use of his skills to escape.

Evidently, Temujin was a man with a sense of self-sufficiency and an instinct to survive. However, for the next three years following his father's death, when he passed away, nobody could imagine the successful leader he was to become. Weatherford believes that Temujin was a frequent cryer and was averse to dogs. He also wasn't as imposing in terms of military expertise. The research suggests that Temujin's younger brother was an archer, wrestler and more powerful. One of his half-brothers was a bully and swore to boss him around (Weatherford 2004).

Temujin's two most important beliefs were the eternal friendship and loyalty. In spite of shame and the scourge of hunger, kidnapping and slaverythat he endured, the Temujin was a believer in the goodwill of the people. One particular boy attracted his attention as a person to befriend for the rest of his life. A teen, who was older, was a friend in his early years. The boy was one who was a man of forever bonded with. Temujin would be doomed to failure. The young boy grew up to become an adult who was his main adversary.

The second connection Temujin created had to do with his wife Borte. Borte was the first wife of Temujin. She was the first to rule the court of Genghis Khan, and was crowned as the grand Empress of Genghis Khan's Empire.

The historical accounts suggest that they were likely to be married in Khan's 13th or 16th years as they got became married at the age of 17 when Borte was just 17. Borte is believed to be born around 1161 which is a year that was prior to Temujin.

It is unclear what happened to the early marriage of Temujin and Borte. The focus is on the reasons why he might have shifted his focus to conquering the world. At the time, the man did not demonstrate any leadership skills. Although the time frame isn't clear but it is well-known that Borte was abducted before Temujin's rise to the ranks.

Temujin, according to scholars, loved his wife just as many people do. He was a fan of the bonds of friendship as well as loyalty. He was able to save himself from the wrath of a rival clan was the result of a mixture of fear and desire. The goal was clear to ensure that his wife was with him.

The abduction was a ploy in members of the Three Mergids clan. They targeted Temujin's family around dawn, according to the historical reports. Temujin as well as the other men that he accumulated were taken off to ride horses and left women in the dust. There was too few horses to carry all the members of his family.

The Merkits were the name was the name of the Three Mergids clan was known as, were the ones who took Borte. Hoelun was kidnapped by the father's tribe of Temujin and this prompted Temujin's father's people to incite the Three Mergids to raid Temujin's camp later on. Hoelun is Temujin's mom. Yesugei took over the Merkits and snatched Hoelun and later Temujin was born.

Temujin was not able to save Borte until eight months later. Temujin teamed up together with Jamukha along with Wang Khan to lead the fight on the Merkits. Temujin was faced with another challenge after he had saved his wife.

The return of Temujin was followed through the birth of a baby. Jochi, the child Jochi could not be Temujin's. The man who captained her kept her in his bed , and may be the father, rather than Temujin. He didn't throw his wife out nor his child and let Jochi remain with the family while claiming him to be his son.

Temujin did produce offspring that clearly reflected his bloodline. Borte was the mother of five daughters and four sons in total. These children were able aid Genghis Khan expand his empire.

Jochi is a member to the same family can not be Genghis Khan's successor. His brothers refused to accept Jochi as their leader because his bloodline wasn't clear. Jochi was appointed as the head for the Golden Horde.

Genghis Khan had additional children by two wives But Borte as his initial wife of the Khan, was granted her title as Grand Empress. The Mongols loved her. In the end, she remained in Mongolia along with Temuge and Temuge, while Genghis traveled across the country conquering. Borte was granted her own land and court to govern. Her sons who were ruled by Genghis Khan, were the only people who were allowed to succeed him.

Temuge was Temujin's older brother, Temujin was the younger brother.

Genghis Khan's Bloodline

In addition to Jochi who had a doubtful genetic lineage Borte had three children: Chagatai Ogedei, Chagatai, and Tolui. Ogedei is Genghis Khan's third son or second, dependent on the extent to which Jochi is considered to be his third son. Ogedei was born around 1186, and later became Genghis Khan's successor. He was responsible for sustaining Genghis Khan's growth to his empire. Mongol Empire south and west. Ogedei was a conqueror of Europe as well as East Asia. Ogedei was also member of his conquests of Iran, China, and Central Asian conquests.

Jochi and Chagatai battled prior to their battle before Khwarezmid Empire invasion in 1219. Ogedei as well as his spouse, who later became the Empress Yisui had a conversation with his Great Khan regarding his future successor. They wanted a name for their successor before the battle. According to the research, Genghis agreed that Ogedei would be his successor after his death.

In confirmation of successors, Tolui served as the civil administrator until 1229, at which point Ogedei was in a position to become the supreme chief of Mongolia. Ogedei's title was elevated to the status of the supreme Khan. He was appointed to the post despite the wishes of his father to have Ogedei succeeding to his position.

It was a custom during the period for Ogedei as the rumored successor to the throne, to be sacked three times before he was declared Khagan, the official name of the Mongols. Genghis Khan is believed to have seen the pragmatism and charisma Ogedei demonstrated as the true ruler and person worthy for succeeding Temujin on the throne.

Chagatai did not go unpunished due to his reckless behavior and struggle with Jochi. He was awarded the majority of what's known as five Central Asian states, upon the death of his father. Chagatai was named the person who would ensure that the Yassa was observed. The Yassa was an unwritten Code of Law, Genghis Khan established after his inauguration as the leader of the Mongol Empire.

Chagatai is considered to be an uncouth and rough son who was addicted to drinking however, he was also an energetic man who had justice within his soul. The scholars agree that Chagatai wasn't the Khan's successor due to his outright rejection of Jochi as the Khan's successor and perhaps Khan's son.

It's a tribute to Genghis Khan's leadership skills that his son's leadership did not immediately destroy the Mongol Empire by fighting with family members about succession. Jochi was not a problem with regard to succession. Jochi died in February 1227 and his father was followed by the month of August in 1227. Jochi left his legacy to his many children. Two daughters and 14 sons are born to Jochi as well as Berke and Tuq-Timur. Both were leaders. Berke was the leader of his golden Horde and Tuq-Timur was in charge of Tuq-Timur's Great Horde. The daughter of Jochi got married to the Oirats.

Genghis Khan was also a father to daughters which were crucial to the growth of Mongolia through marriage. Khochen Bekhi, the oldest daughter, and she got married to Senggum who was the grandson of Wang Khan. She also got married to Botu.

Alakhai Bekhi also went through several marriages. She was a part of her tribe, the Ongut tribe, and later married the chieftain's nephew. And her final wedding was with Boyaohe, her stepson.

Tumelun married Chigu. Chigu was the child of Anchen and Dei Seichen, the father of Borte. Alaltun was married to Olar from the Olkhunut tribe. She also got married to an stepson, Taichu, and later got married to Uyghur idiqut. Checheikhen was Checheikhen's last daughter of the couple who got wed Torolchi which was part of the Oirat tribe.

Genghis Khan also had children by his various wives. Genghis Khan had 11 wives, with some of them traveling with him frequently and others who received little note in the history books. Khulan Khatun, Yesugen Khatun And Yesulun Khataun Three of his wife who have made an impact in the histories. Khulan was the leader of his second court, and she was the second wife after Borte. She was in his court during the Khwarezmid Empire's conquer. Yesugen and Yesugen along with Yesulun have their own court, however none of the power Khan's wives were members within the Mongol Empire.

Genghis Khan Facts About his early life

* Temujin began to increase in his influence at the age of 20 four years after the day he got married Borte.

* At the age of 20 He was seized and imprisoned for a brief period of time.

At the age of 20 years old, Khan was already building one of the best army forces around the globe, accumulating more than 20,000 soldiers.

* His bloodline assisted him to overcome Asia and lead the Mongol Empire beginning in 1206.

* It is widely believed that, at the start in the Mongol Empire, Temujin became Genghis Khan.

* He passed away in August 1227, just seven months after the birth of his "first" child was born, Jochi.

* Jochi was believed to be intoxicated by an assassin.

Chapter 3: The Bekhter's Death And The Backlash

Imagine being a child approaching the age of marriage and knowing that the death of your dad was caused by an adversary. If you felt rejected by your peers, enduring hardship and suffering from bullying You might consider looking at acceptable ways of life around you to get some guidance.

Temujin's home was not an ideal one. It was broken , and it was getting more deteriorating. But, there was an element of Temujin's conduct that began to demonstrate that the world that he was a smart leader.

There was always conflict regarding hunts. Bekhter the half-brother of Temujin was a constant target of his bullies and it was believed that he attempted to take one of his parents. Bekhter was definitely trying to keep food in his own kitchen and not share it with the entire family members who were struggling.

It was evident from the actions of these men that Bekhter would only live for himself , regardless of the needs of those around him.

A tradition in Mongolia was prevalent in the time. It was commonplace for male children to marry the wife of their father, provided that they did not have a mother. Because Bekhter was born to an entirely different mother and same father it was appropriate to have him marry the mother of Temujin's. By marrying Hoelun, Bekhter would have become the family lord and Temujin's son would have become the new father.

This was did not sit well with Temujin because of Bekhter's self-centeredness. To determine the family tree Temujin was a child of the father's previous wife , and therefore the most obvious successor.

The drawback was that he had to reach 15 years old before he could be considered seriously as the father's tribe. Temujin did not want Bekhter marrying his mother. He needed to take action to make sure that Bekhter could not be in the position to assume the family. Bekhter is also older and so he was able to marry Temujin's mom before Temujin was 15 and took on his role.

Temujin is captured

Despite his moral reasons to safeguard his family and his desire to become a clan leader however, the Mongols did not have a favorable view on his conduct. Murder, regardless of the motive and especially against the rules of proper succession, was a fact. Many tribes were angry by the actions of Temujin and didn't let him go unpunished.

At the margins of society Temujin was wanted by the Taichiut tribe to retaliate against the tribe for his actions. The tribe swarmed into the camp, and seized Temujin as well as the brothers who assisted in killing Bekhter. After being initially detained, Temujin was able to escape before being detained a second time.

Temujin was not able to escape the second time. It's unclear whether the Taichuit were responsible for the attack. The history is a bit sparse regarding these matters. But, whatever transpired to him in the time were in prison certain to give him the desire for a union of all the Mongol tribes and to lead them to a better life with better ethical and legal standards than what the ones he was made to live with.

Aspects of the 11th Century in Asia

Numerous studies have done on Asian cultures which includes Mongolia. Mongols were firmly based on the patriarchal system. The wives were taken into clans to be married to sons. Daughters were taken to be married to different clans. Clans that gave wives were thought to be more powerful, whereas those that married their wives were thought to be less powerful.

If sons were married they were entitled to some in the household's riches that was the livestock and their sheep. The rules changed after Genghis Khan ruled the empire. Genghis Khan created the Yassa however, instead of analyzing the Yassa it is essential to comprehend the code that he was expected to adhere to.

Sons replace fathers, typically the oldest son in the event of an issue of lineage. Men could have any number of wives they wanted, but the first wife was the one who ruled over the others. Women were able to exercise authority in their own right. For instance, Borte had her own court and the territory. The first wife was able to resolve legal issues during the absence of her husband.

Although women were thought of as powerful by men but they were also used as used as tools. Women were used to marry to clan members that were suitable. If a clan marriage could be arranged, and so the clan was protected, women were required to get married.

Women who were left behind would be subjected to their master and given a new home or even raped when they were not able to adhere to the rules of the new clan.

Evidently, slavery was a problem. Clans that fight could make sure that group of members from a rival clan who do not make use of them, and not simply requiring subjugation. If a child is in tension, and with a desire for goals, preparing his mind a plan for a better life Temujin is likely to have begun to plan.

Temujin's Plot

Temujin was forced to plan an escape plan to free himself from his captors. There are many legends about how this took place. The most plausible story claims that this man was confined in a yurt but was managed to escape while nobody was watching. He was probably around fourteen at that time which makes it possible that he could have studied, learned and studied the clan around him , and then managed to escape.

This is most likely since Temujin then, later Genghis Khan was able to eliminate massive hordes that were larger than his army because he was one of the most effective warlords who could be considered strategic in the history of.

Temujin was aware that he could accomplish absolutely nothing without assistance. He was still loyal as his primary requirement with clan members. He knew that making alliances to strengthen his position was essential. However, his family was on the fringes society, and he was responsible for the murder of Bekhter. In order to gain power, he must be savvy and build alliances that would secure long-term commitments from the Mongols.

Chapter 4: Genghis Khan's Rise To Power

The very first thing Temujin did after becoming liberated from slavery was to search for Borte and to get married. The betrothal was in place from the age of nine. Borte's father was a member of the tribe, and was also in good terms with his tribe. He was married to ensure that the existence of at least two tribes to back his back, providing him with the power needed to be able to rule his clan.

The accounts from the past of Genghis Khan's early years show that he was young but he had ideas about how to boost his power. Evidently, gaining the ranks of power would not be an easy task. It will require a amount of intelligence, but the details of his rise to power proved that he was blessed with the ability to be more knowledgeable than the average person of his age.

It is possible that his experience on the margins of power, and society helped him understand the areas where society was failing the Mongols. The time he spent in slavery may also have taught him about military skills, and how crucial having good relations between clans could assist him to attain the power he wanted.

Injustice is a method of strengthening those who feel truly wronged and possess the character to lead. Genghis Khan is one them. In his quest to be a great man and perhaps even tyranny Genghis Khan made use of the resources at his disposal.

Borte gave him two clans as a result of his wedding. One was the Borte clan. He also managed to create an alliance making use of his or her mother's wedding present. A luxury coat was given on his mother or himself There are a variety of accounts of this. He presented the coat and presented it to Keraits head, Toghril Ongkhan. This was a decision which helped him establish an affiliation with one of most powerful clans in the region.

Toghril was one of the people Temujin might have considered an all-around ally. Toghril's father was also a person with whom Toghril were blood brothers in relationship. Toghril was often restored to his throne through the assistance from Temujin's dad.

It is possible Temujin believed that Toghril was equally important as his father Temujin.

Temujin probably believed that Toghril should be respectful to Temujin.

But, for a man who wanted to be a leader and improve the world environment, Temujin was able to take his decisions fast, and sometimes too quickly. He was determined to enforce his ideas, and control larger areas, and it caused a lot of anger among other tribes.

Jamuqa

Jamuqa or Jamukha according to the source, was believed to be as a blood brother to Temujin's. He was his closest friend from childhood; he pledged allegiance to him before his slavery. Researchers, archeologists and other scholars think that Temujin stayed for a several years or more Jamuqa to get to know more about the military and political methods of Mongolia. Jamuqa was an older man and, at the time, willing to share his knowledge.

The Merkit

The mystery surrounding Borte's kidnapping is not fully understood in relation to the reason she was able to be left behind. According to some sources, Genghis Khan was forced to defend himself first before he could protect his wife. There was also a sense of panic and that in the attack, the woman was left to fend for herself. But, as it turned out and the humiliation he hurled at Temujin for having his wife taken away and making her the spouse of the Merkit leader allowed Temujin to display his power that he acquired.

Temujin was not able to find enough men to save his wife. In the end, he had go towards Jamuqa or Toghril. The two tribal leaders been able to form an alliance with Temujin as was stated earlier.

The luck may have been on the side of Temujin. Toghril was not a fan of the Merkit according to the experts. It's quite possible Toghril was eager to reap benefits from helping Temujin in addition to paying the old debt.

Toghril and Jamuqa were able to take down the Merkit and Temujin's assistance. Borte was captured while the Merkits were not able to save their tribe.

Temujin at this point in the present, had some help and a lot of determination. Experts such as Weatherford believe that Temujin knew some of the potential of alliances however the kidnapping and murder of Borte was really the turning stage. He realized the power he was able to have against the power that other people were always able to exert over him.

It is possible that Temujin, who was now aware of the power of alliances, realized it was necessary to build new relationships with other tribes. However, as an adolescent, just past 16 years old, it was possible to be viewed as insignificant and too young to those who really wanted to be on his side.

Utilizing Anyone Temujin Could

It was following the recovery of Borte that Temujin went on to spend an entire year or more with Jamuqa. For Temujin it wasn't all about friendship but rather the value of. Jamuqa was seen as an exceptional leader, especially on the battlefields. Temujin was not old enough to be able to experience this. It's evident that Temujin mastered tactical awareness of the battlefield as well as military strategies.

Many details about this time of Temujin's existence were disregarded. Researchers have put together the information they could and speculated on other ideas. It was known that as the time when Jamuqa and Temujin's blood brothers started to strain and finally break up, a large portion members of the Jamuqa tribe were amazed by Temujin.

They were so impressed that they decided to move away from Jamuqa's tribe to Temujin's Tribe. Borjigin.

It is this shift of his supporters that tells us the power of Temujin's charisma. If there wasn't any sense of charisma, intelligence or leadership in Temujin's ranks, he could not have built one of the most powerful empires of all time in only two short years.

Professor Weatherford's research on A Secret History, believes Temujin was not sure about breaking his ties with Jamuqa. The shift in Jamuqa in refusing to share his power , and in treating Temujin as less than him was, was that was confusing for Temujin.

At the time, he was barely 19. He had much to master and confront. Weatherford says it was Borte who aided in making her husband's choice. She was not Hoelun his mother who advised them to break up the next time Jamuqa established camp.

It was either by plan or luck, Temujin was able to win over a lot of Jamuqa's supporters. They did steal many of the cattle and horses. In the beginning, Jamuqa didn't pursue Temujin. Maybe, if one wants to imagine it as if Jamuqa did not forget the friendship with Temujin, his brother blood. It is more likely that Jamuqa was not convinced that Temujin would ever achieve such a position.

Over the span of 20 years, both Temujin as well as Jamuqa both gained strength. They fought against with each other and lost men, women and even goods to one and creating new alliances and gaining immense power. In 1189, despite their efforts to unite all the Mongol tribes, both sides were unable to achieve this. The legends and the records indicate that Temujin attempted to satisfy his desire through a final battle against Jamuqa and himself. Jamuqa.

The Khuriltai

There was a Khuriltai. Khuriltai is a council which was used to support Khans. People who attended could vote for Temujin. And when no one turned up or just a handful others were present the result was that Jamuqa was still more powerful than Temujin.

There is no evidence of a document, it is evident that Temujin didn't get the backing he was hoping for. He also remained allied with the Borte tribe as a subject rather than being a Khan. Ong Khan was willing that Temujin should try to unify his two Mongol tribes.

It is possible that Ong Khan was not convinced that unification of the tribe was a significant enough reason to worry about. Maybe it was his wish to concede so that Temujin as well as Jamuqa continued to fight one another instead of trying to be above the Kereyid who was a far larger tribe.

Rise To Power

With incredible partners and his own personal power Temujin led the Merkit with the help of a system that Temujin was usually to slash the seeds of insubordination to come. He vowed never to let any adversary behind and, years later prior to the assault on China the first time, he'd make sure that no traveler chief committed a crime for betraying him. Soon after the destruction of the Merkit and the

Jurkin faction, he regarded his respectability for the Jurkin group in the same manner. They, as the best of his co-rulers, had benefited from his inability to attend an attack on the Tatars to take his possessions. Temujin wiped out the honorability of the group and accepted ordinary citizens as his soldiers and employees. When his abilities had grown enough to permit him to take on an ultimatum against the massive Tatars He initially defeated the Tatars in a battle and then slayed each of them to a height greater than the height of a truck's pivot. The children could be counted on to become unaware of their previous character and eventually become loyal followers to the Mongols. When the alliance between the Kereit and Toghril from the Kereit was finally dissolved and Temujin required to remove the obstacle to a formidable force, he swathed the Kereit members with the Mongols as soldiers and workers. The heartlessness of this group was not desire for cold-bloodedness. Temujin had a plan to kill any of the previous blue-blooded rivals, who could be an obstruction point and to grant himself a fighting power and, more importantly, to increase the sense of tribal loyalty that favored discontinuity, and to be a part of the wanderers who were in close-to-home compliance with his family. In addition, when, 1206 was the year he came to be recognized as the king of all steppe people, he had the power to transfer a vast amount of families to the care of his relatives and friends and replace the present system of clans and groups by something that was more of a primitive arrangement.

In any case, from the time of the demise of the Merkits Temujin had his eyes on the incredible things that happened in the steppes to himself. The new friendship with Jamuka continued for just 18 months. At time, while the two were out walking, Jamuka expressed a baffling comment regarding the decision of the camp, which prompted Temujin's partner Borte to convince him to decide that it was the right time for them to set out towards their destination. The story behind this moment is not clear. The tale of The Secret History is excessively confusing in its brevity and subdued language, which makes it difficult to provide an accurate clarification. It is believed that Jamuka was trying to trigger an outbreak of the plan. In the same way, it could happen that Jamuka's language was deliberately dark in order to ignore the fact that Temujin was likely to leave his friend. However, Temujin accepted Borte's recommendation. Many of Jamuka's men have also left him, probably watching the character of Temujin the man they thought was likely to prevail at end. In the Secret History legitimizes their activity in dramatic terms. One of the men informs Temujin that a dream was shown to him, and has to be understood to mean it was the case that Heaven and Earth were in agreement that Temujin was the ruler of the realm. When you examine the situation in a more sensible way, the interactions of the shifting loyalties of the steppe could be seen. The clansmen were aware of what was happening and some were quick to join Temujin's side. They knew that a solid leader was coming and that it would be logical to declare for him in the right moment.

The conflict with Jamuka resulted in a polarization within the Mongol world that could be resolved with the disappearance of one of the enemies. Jamuka is not a promotor ever. In the Secret History has a lot to say about him, but not always in a way that is empathetically but it's the story of the Temujin family as well as Jamuka appears as the enemy, though occasionally the latter is a bit hesitant. He's a conundrum an individual with enough strength of personality to lead an adversarial alliance of sovereigns and choose gur-khan, or an incomparable khan, to be chosen in their favor. But he was also an inquisitive, a person who was quick to judge of things, willing to let go of his comrades, or even turn against them to gain a quick profit. For Temujin it could be in Jamuka's power to take on the Mongols but Temujin was the most well-known man and his competition ended up breaking Jamuka.

The Tribe pioneers began to gather them at Temujin and Jamuka and, in the years before the turn century, a number of them suggested to create Temujin Khan one of the Mongols. The way they described it as such, urging him to show dedication to war and in the pursuit, advise that all they were looking for was a trustworthy general, not the overlord they wanted him to transform into. It is certain that later, certain of them would leave him. In fact, at present Temujin was only one of the minor chieftains as shown by the subsequent significant incident that is described in The Secret History, a fight at a dinner party, provoked by his supposed partners, his Jurkin sovereigns, who were later killed by him. The

Jin head of the northern part of China was also watched him from afar, with not a remarkable result. One of strategy inversions typical for their control over their wandering companions, Jin assaulted their onetime allies the Tatars. With Toghril, Temujin held onto the possibility of pursuing the faction dispute and then sacked the Tatars to the back. The Jin sovereign compensated Toghril through his Chinese name of Wang which means ruler. He also offered Temujin a less enlightened one. In reality it was not for any time, Jin was not in danger from Temujin. He was fully engaged in building his strength in the steppe and was no obvious danger to China.

Temujin has now set about to eliminate all his opponents. The progressive alliances created by Jamuka were defeated. The Tatars were destroyed. Toghril allowed himself to be drawn by the desires of Jamuka as well as his own child's dreams and doubts into an extensive conflict against Temujin and Kereit's Kereit people were wiped out. In the west there was the Naiman ruler, scared of the growing ferocity of the Mongols was attempting to create another alliance, based on the desire of Jamuka but was utterly crushed and his realm was destroyed. Jamuka was as mutable as it could be, left the Naiman Khan at last. The crusades took place a few years prior to 1206 and made Temujin the as the ace in the steppes. In that year , an extraordinary gathering was held along on the River Onon, and Temujin was declared Genghis Khan. The title could mean the Universal Ruler.

The Unification of The Mongol Nation

1206 was a pivotal year throughout the history of Mongols and throughout the history of the world The second year was when the Mongols were the first to venture out beyond the steppe. Mongolia changed its form. The nil-inspiring combats and fights were an epoch from the past. It is possible that the well-known clan and group names were wiped out of use or the names carrying them were to be discovered, thus scattered across all over the Mongol world, and proving the disaster zone of the traditional faction as well as the clan structure. The abounding Mongol country was seen as the personal creation of Genghis Khan. It has undergone many modifications (primitive crumbling and early retribalization, the provincial occupation) is now thriving to the present day. Mongol desire was a step beyond the steppe. Genghis Khan was set to embark on his incredible journey of global success. The new nation was planned out, but most importantly, to be ready for the war. Genghis Khan's troops were divided according to the decimal framework. They were unable to move and well-equipped and supplied. The commanding officers were his children or his chosen men who were completely loyal to him.

Genghis Khan's military genius was able to adapt to rapidly changing conditions. In the beginning, his soldiers were solely mounted that rode the sturdy grass-took Mongol horse, which didn't require grain. With this kind of army the different migrant communities could be wiped out, but urban communities could not be destroyed. After a brief period after which the Mongols could choose to take on massive urban communities by using mangonels, slings, stool, eating oil and, always taking over streams. It was simply a step by step, in contact with the men of more settled states that Genghis Khan came to realize that there were newer methods of gaining a boost without a lot of crushing, attacking, and destruction. The priest from the khan of Naiman, the final significant Mongol clan that opposed Genghis Khan, who taught his the benefits of education, and reduced the significance of the Mongol language to writing. The Secret History states that it was merely following the war against the Muslim kingdom of Khwarezm located in the region in the region of Amu Darya (Oxus) and Syr Darya (Jaxartes) probably around the end of 1222 Genghis Khan learned from Muslim advice on the "significance and importance cities." It was another advisor at some point in the past under an administration under Jin, the Jin leader, that explained to him the work of specialists and workers in the production of assessable goods. He proposed to turn the fertile fields of northern China into food-producing fields to feed his horses.

The amazing victories of the Mongols that would transform them into a political power nation, would be yet to be. China was their primary goal. Genghis Khan had previously secured that his western flank was protected with a fierce battle against the Tangut kingdom of Xixia which was a northern outskirt province in China which was later encroached on the Jin domain in northwestern China during 1211. In 1214, he allowed himself to be paid in a short time, by an enormous amount of goods. However, the work was not stopped until 1215 as well as Beijing was removed. In this way, the most effective persecution in northern China was under the control of Muqali, his general. Genghis Khan was himself compelled to deviate away from China and win the war of Khwarezm. The war was provoked by the head of the legislature of Otrar, the city's legislative head. Otrar who killed the parade of Muslim vendors under Genghis Khan's protection. The Khwarezm-Shah resisted fulfillment. The war with Khwarezm is likely to be a possibility at one time or another, however, at the moment it was not possible to end it. In this war, the Mongols were able to gain fame due to their brutality and fear. Every city was attacked by the people who were killed or forced to serve as advance soldiers for Mongols against their relatives. Gardens and fields were destroyed and water systems destroyed in the course of Genghis Khan sought to impose his uncompromising retaliation against the famous city of Khwarezm. Genghis Khan finally was able to retreat in 1223, and didn't take his army into battle again until the end of the battle against Xixia between 1226 and 1227. He died on the 18th of August 1227.

Inheritance

In the sense that it can be determined from disparate source, Genghis Khan's character was an enigma. He was a physical marvel with incredible strength determination, determination, and an unbreakable determination. He was never settled and would listen to advice from other people such as his spouse and mother. He was able to adapt. He was adept at tricking, yet not overly impressive. He felt the level of trustworthiness which was far from Toghril and Jamuka. Anyone who was guilty of a foul act towards their masters would be able to expect quick action from him, yet they would be able to exploit their unfairness at the same time. He was highly disapproved as a result of his sense of an ideal crucial moment and in moments of crisis He would reverence his Eternal Blue Heaven as well as the incomparable divine power in the Mongols. The same is true in his early life. The reality of his life becomes less friendly as he steps beyond his circle of familiarity and is entangled with the strange, settled world that lies beyond the steppe. From the beginning it was difficult for him to comprehend the rapid profits that can be made from rapine or slaughter, and, at times was consumed by a desire for revenge. In the course of his existence, he was able to draw into the trust of those who were willing to help him, including individuals who were displaced and the socially minded men from the world of settled people. The acclaim he received could influence the older Daoist master Changchun (Qiu Chuji) to travel across the entire across Asia to meet with him on specific questions. He was an all-round versatile person as a person who could be taught.

Order, association mobility, and savagery of the direction were among the primary elements in his victories. The slaying of the population and the resulting dread was a weapon he frequently used. His strategy of calling urban areas to surrender and organizing the systematic slaughter of those who refused to surrender is portrayed as a mental fight; however, in the same way while it was no doubt an ounce of doubt a strategy to eliminate the opposition by fostering fear however, the killing was used to benefit the individual. Mongol practice, especially during the battle against Khwarezm was to send out specialists to disperse and isolate an troops and the inhabitants of a city that was in conflict by blending threats with the assurance of. The Mongols are known for their brutality. often killed their prisoners who allowed themselves to be killed when resistance or escape was definitely possible. In fact they were Mongols were inaccessible. Obstruction was a sure way to end their reign However, at Balkh the moment it is in Afghanistan the population was murdered despite a quick abandonment, due to strategic reasons.

The achievements from Genghis Khan were impressive. Genghis Khan was part of the numerous clans of the clans traveling around, and using military capabilities that were mediocre in numbers, he destroyed incredible realms like, Khwarezm and the considerably impressive Jin state. But he did not deplete his clan. He selected the replacement for him, his son Ogodei with great consideration and a promise that his various children would follow Ogodei and gave him a military as well as an undisputed state. In the time of his death, Genghis Khan had vanquished the entire landmass stretching from Beijing up to his home in the Caspian Sea, and his officers had fought Persia as well as Russia. His successors would extend their power over all region of China, Persia, and the majority of Russia. They achieved what he couldn't do and may never have had in mind, namely, to weave their successes into a organized and regulated area. The destruction wrought by Genghis Khan has a place in not-so-popular memory, yet significant, these victories aren't the sole period of the Mongol Empire, which was the most successful mainland kingdom of medieval and even modern-day.

The rise of Genghis Khan

It was within Mongolia at the time that Genghis Khan (his real name was Temuujin) was born in 1162 (the date that is cited by current Mongol research). Temuujin came from a tribe which had a culture of force and discipline and was the remarkable grandchild of Khabul (Qabul) Khan, who was the greatest commander among All the Mongols. Temuujin was involved in a dispute with the Juchen-Jin administration, and a second one against the Tatars who had been able to double-cross an insurance precursor from his family to Juchen. His father was hurt by the Tatars. There were also disputes among the factions that made up All the Mongols and a dispute with the revolutionary Merkit (Mergid) family which his father had taken his mother.

*

*

Temuujin was abandoned in his teens. His family was afflicted by terrible times, and his force to the Mongols were spread across different tribes. Even in such simple practices as camp strike and ponies stealing and stealing, he successfully employed traditional practices like marriage unions; placing himself in the hands of a more rational ruler; and forming an alliance against Jamuka (later his feared adversary) through promising anda in which the two men became like a kindred spirit; and deciding on the nokhor ("mates"). This was not at all as a result of the anda system that created an imagined familial connection and posed the possibility of a dangerous conflict A man who transformed into a nokhor, renounced all ties to connections and clan and declared himself "the person" of his chosen the pioneer.

Genghis Khan later left as a nokhor, however the nokhor never got him traded by a nokhor. his greatest commandos were nokhors.

In 1206 his accomplishment in the inborn fight led him to become the chief for All the Mongols with the status of khan, and the title Genghis (Chinggis)-the word derived from the Turkic tengizwhich means "sea" Although this clarification hasn't persuaded everyone Mongol researcher, it's solidly based on the idea that the sea was a symbol of the vastness and shrewdness of the Mongols. (Later the same Mongol term Dalai was used to refer to the most renowned lama in Tibet.) The previous travelers have been able to attack China but none of them could have resisted the entire country, mostly due to their rash attacks leaving other wanderers in their midst and to their rear. Genghis Khan may, if you might, was the first to join all the Tuurgatan ("individuals of the tents with felt walls") in a test farther back, away from China in order to make sure that they controlled any wandering adversaries.

The first step was to handle the most important ancestral gatherings to his west in Mongolia The Naiman along with Kereit

(Kerait) and Kereit (Kerait) who he was again at war and in contention like the clans that bordered Siberia and Mongolia in the north. Then he began to move towards the eastern region in northern China (at the time, controlled by Jin administration Jin administration) towards the south, almost all the way to Yangtze River (Chang Jiang). In the northwestern part of China and in the western part of Inner Mongolia, there was an expressway, which was is part of Xi (Western) Xia. The rulers of the Xi Xia included Tangut from Tibet and under their rule was a number of Turkish as well as Sogdian dealers who made a mess of the parade exchange. The people who cultivated those desert hot springs included Turks along with Chinese. China that was south of Yangtze was ruled through the Nan (Southern) Song tradition (1127-1279). Although they lost North China, the Nan Song were expanding southward towards Indochina and brought rich new areas in development. Within each of these states there was an exchange of deliberation, coalitions formed and broken, and also open combat.

Between 1207-1215, the military of Genghis Khan delved deep to North China. Genghis

Khan utilised the Khitan in the north and northeastern regions of China who Liao tradition Jin was toppled and were now malcontented subordinates of Jin. In 1215, the Jin capital Zhongdu (present-day Beijing), from where Zhongdu, the Jin ruler had retreated towards the south, was taken and destroyed. In any event, acknowledging that it was not the right time to pledge his fundamental support to the victory of China, Genghis Khan pulled back to Mongolia leaving the most powerful large, Mugali, to attack and cripple the nation. He turned westward. When his hammer had smashed the Naiman as well as the rest of the clans of incredible strength in Mongolia legitimate, including the child of the final leader of this clan Kuchlug was forced to flee Karakhitai and tied the knot with the tiny girl of its previous ruler, whom he overthrew. In the realm of a variety that included Semirechie located in Russian Turkistan and the Kashgar (Kashi) desert located in Chinese Turkistan (present-day Xinjiang) Kuchlug was a supporter of his Buddhist minority and was a snob to Islam as a major part of the religion. This was a reason for Mongols to eliminate him. It was the Mongol General Jebe declared a time of religious freedom and banned slaughter and looting. This indicates that the Mongols didn't kill out of pure brutality, but only when they realized that it was important to weaken the power of an opponent.

In assuming control over the land in Karakhitai, the assuming of control over Karakhitai opened the way to Genghis Khan's journey to Khwarezm in the region that is famous for its desert springs that flow along the Amu Darya (old Oxus River) which is now Turkmenistan along with Uzbekistan. This provided him with a possibility against China as well as secured him from the threat of another traveling power organizing along his flank and to his back, a striking force supported by urban and agrarian assets. Once this was accomplished and completed, he retreated in toward China and left the further trek towards Russia as well as the Eastern regions and the eastern outskirts of Europe to his superiors and their children. He wouldn't be as in the sense that he could surrender to the principal power of China until he was able to manage the prosperous Tangut Province that was Xi Xia, and it was during this enlightened mission in 1227 when he dropped the bucket.

The Yuan or Mongol custom

The Mongol victory over China

Genghis Khan achieved a matchless excellence against the Mongol clans of the steppes beginning in 1206 and within two years, he attempted to take on northern China. In 1209 the commitment to his Tangut region in Xi (Western) Xia in the areas that are now Gansu, Ningxia, and areas from Shaanxi and Qinghai in the process, he eliminated the possibility of a possible adversary and set the terrain for an attack against the Jin state of Juchen of northern China. At that time, the history of Jin was questioned. The Juchen were exhausted through a costly conflict (1206-08) with their genetic enemies they were the Nan (Southern) Song. Unrest among the nation-Juchen elements of the Jin people (Chinese as well as Khitan) was growing to the point that a few from Chinese or Khitan nobles fled for their Mongol side. Genghis Khan, as he prepared his preparations for the battle against Jin was able to at this point rely on distant counsellors who were knowledgeable about the region and States that comprised that Jin state.

The Jin state is under attack. Jin state

The Mongol military began their offensive in 1211, and began to attack from the north, in three separate gatherings; Genghis Khan drove the inside gatherings himself. For a long time, they destroyed the country; finally 1214, they turned their attention on the capital city that was Jin, Zhongdu (present-day Beijing). The strongholds of Jin proved difficult to withstand, and the Mongols completed their peace and retreated. In the flash of an eye, a and a half later, the Jin ruler made his way towards the capital of the southern region at Bianjing (present-day Kaifeng). Genghis Khan saw this as a violation of the truce and his charged assault brought large chunks from northern China to Mongol control. The last of this was 1215 with the capture from Zhongdu (renamed Dadu in 1272). The Mongols did not have any involvement in fighting in areas with a large population Their strength was predominantly in mounted force attacks. The aid by deserters of the Jin state probably contributed to this initial Mongol success. The Mongols were heavily dependent on the varied abilities and methods of the growing amount of Chinese that they influenced.

After 1215, Jin was reduced to a minor support state that was a little support state between Mongols to the north, in the north and Song China in the south and their destruction was an extremely short period. The Mongol fights against Xi Xia in 1226-27 and Genghis Khan's death in 1227 caused a short time of peace for Jin but the Mongols continued to fight until 1230.

The Song Chinese, seeing an opportunity to gain back a piece of the areas they lost to Juchen during the twelfth century, formed a coalition along with Mongols and launched an attack on Bianjing around 1232. Aizong one of the rulers in Jin was forced to leave Bianjing in 1233 just before the city's fall and was moved in Cai Prefecture (Henan) but the asylum was also condemned. In 1234, the ruler dissolved his reign, and the opposition was stopped. The southern part of the former Jin express, the Huai River, is now turning into the border of the Mongol domains in the north of China.

The attack from the Song state

Over the next few decades, uneasy alliances were formed between the Mongols in the north of China along with in the Song state in south. The Mongols developed further in

1250 under the dazzling Khalifa Mongke and his younger brother Kublai Khan, who were the grandsons of Genghis Khan. Their military outsmarted the principal Song protections along the Yangtze River and entered profoundly into southwest China and defeated the independent Dai (Tai) area of Nanzhao (in the area that is now Yunnan) and reached the the present-day northern Vietnam. Mongke passed away in 1259, while driving the military to take an Song Fortifications in Sichuan and Kublai succeeded the throne. Kublai had an official, Hao Jing, to the Song court with the idea to create a harmonious relationship. Hao was not able to reach the Song capital city of Lin'an (presently Hangzhou), in spite, however, he was interned on the outskirts and was regarded as a simple official. It was the Song Chancellor Jia Sidao, considered the Song position to be able to take on this insult against Kublai. In this way missed the chance to make peace with Kublai, instead attempting to make sure that the military arrangements were strengthened against a possible Mongol attack. Jia was able to ensure the security of military arrangements with changing the land that involved taking land from owners with huge wealth however this was a step back for the majority of the landowners and the authority class. It was the Song officers, who Jia asked questions about, also were unhappy, which could explain why some of their officers later surrendered their land to Mongols without fighting.

Cai WenjiA Mongol settlement Detail taken from Cai Wenji look-over A Chinese hand-look from the Nan (Southern) Song dynasty. Photo courtesy of Asia Society Galleries, New York

From 1267 onwards, From 1267 to 1268, the Mongols with the help by numerous Chinese specialists and assistant soldiers experts, fought on several areas. The town of the prefectural located in Xiangyang (present-day Xianfan) on the Han River was a key post that blocked the entry for the Yangtze River, and the Mongols took over the town for a considerable period (1268-73). The Chinese administrator finally quit in 1273, after having received a significant assurance by the Mongols to help the people and then he was able to cooperate with his former enemies.

Kublai Khan's warning to his powers to not engage in a ruthless slaughter seems to have been given attention to in part. A few prefectures along the Yangtze River gave up; other were removed following short battles. In January 1276 Mongol soldiers landed in Lin'an. The very late efforts of the Song court to conclude an agreement failed and Mongol army captured Lin'an on February. The ruling Song sovereign dame as well as the apparent ruler, a boy, were brought to Dadu and offered a large number of people to Kublai Khan.

The national opposition within the Song state continued however it was, and the supporters were forced to withdraw with two sovereigns to the south of Fujian and then to the territory that is now Guangzhou (Canton). In 1277 , the last remnants of the court departed Guangzhou and ultimately left the region via pontoon. A uncompromising priest killed himself and the final enduring magnificent sovereign at sea in the month of March in 1279. When the sorted out any opposition was stopped after remote trespassers ruled the entire Chinese kingdom without precedent in the history of.

China is now under Mongols

Mongol government and its organization

Following their successes in northern China in the years 1211-15 The Mongols faced the challenge of how to control and remove benefits from the greatest extent stationary population. They were assisted with the help of Khitan and Chinese as well as Juchen mavericks. The deserters were regarded as "friends" (nokor) to Mongols. Mongols and were granted positions similar to the more prestigious positions of the steppe, which was privileged. Their advantages were derived from the management and abuse of fiefs that were considered to be their personal space.

Early Mongol standard

The framework for administration during the first few years of the Mongol victory was a mixture of Mongol military structure and the constant return to Chinese practices in the spaces that were governed by the previous members from the Jin state. The most important office or capability of the Mongol organization was Darughatchi (seal conveyor) which was initially comprehensive. only step-by-step were sub-functions assigned to distinct officials as per Chinese the bureaucratic convention. The re-feudalization process of the northern region of China and northern China, in accordance with Mongol patterns, with a slight substructure of Chinese civil servants, continued for a considerable period of time.

The primary structure in Mongol China was in large part the creation of Yelu Chucai. He was initially an official of the Jin state authority with Khitan origin who had received an important Chinese grant and had received the Genghis Khan's close advisors. Yelu continued to serve under the leadership of Ogodei who was made a great Khan in 1229. He encouraged him to establish an established organization and replace the endless tolls with an appropriate tax assessment system based on Chinese models. One of the most significant aspects of Yelu's modifications was the creation of the Central Secretariat (Zhongshu Sheng) that brought together the common citizen organizations and achieved some consistency. The domain was divided into regions, and regular organizations were accountable to regular tax assessment. Individuals were required to settle the land charge as well as an assessment charge or in cash (materials and grains) and in gold. The traders had to pay on a business cost. The business models for vinegar, wine salt, salt, and mining products were also presented. This allowed the Treasury that were held by the Mongol court to accumulate incredible riches.

In spite of the success of his financial arrangement Yelu's influence diminished in his latter years. One reason is a significant limitation from the Mongol feudatories as well as from the Chinese, Juchen, and Khitan nobles, who were used to managing themselves independently in their aprons and who abused their power in a voluntary manner. In addition, Ogodei himself lost enthusiasm towards the inner states of that Mongol territories in China. In the 1230s, Muslims of in the Middle East had just started to fill in the vacancies in the Mongol court and their ruthless use of Chinese led to a wide-ranging hatred for the Mongol traditional. A relapse into chaos primitive was inevitable and the changes of Yelu were sucked into a permanent control. China was governed as a settlement by outsiders and their associates.

The changes Under Kublai Khan and his replacements

Kublai Khan's power in 1260 was a clear shift in Mongol government practices. Kublai relocated the headquarters of the Mongol government from Karakorum located in Mongolia and moved it to Shangdu ("Upper Capital") near to the opening of Day Dolun to Inner Mongolia. In 1267, the capital of the Mongols was relocated to Zhongdu which is in which Kublai demanded the construction of another walled city, filled with stunning royal residences as well as authorities quarters. The city was later renamed Dadu ("Great Capital") before it was built. With the Turkicized title, Cambaluc (Khan-baliq, "The Khan's Town") The capital became known across Asia as well as Europe. In any case, consistent with traveler conventions, the Mongol court kept on moving between these two living arrangements--Shangdu in summer and Dadu in winter. Since the establishment of Dadu as the capital of the central administrative structure, Mongolia and Karakorum no were any longer the mainstays for Karakorum, the heart of Mongol realm. Mongolia was able to return to its position as the northern borderland. the lifestyle of a wanderer continued and Mongol greats were dissatisfied with the growing Sinicization of the court, became always occupied themselves with uprisings.

Kublai was a man who, even before 1260 was required to surround himself in a circle of Chinese guides, including famed Buddho-Daoist Liu Bingzhong and a couple of other Jin researchers were the official ruler of other Mongol areas (ulus) within Asia. At that time, in all likelihood Kublai's Chinese company was convincing him to accept the role of a traditional Chinese sovereign. An important step forward was taken in 1271, when it was 1271 that the Chinese domain was granted the Chinese Dynastic name, Da Yuan, known as the "Incomparable origin." Prior to this was it was believed that the Chinese term of the Mongol state was Da Chao ("Great Dynasty") which was introduced around 1217. It was a reinterpretation to the Mongol name, Yeke Mongghol Ulus ("Great Mongol Nation") which was embraced by Genghis Khan, who was born in 1206. The name change however, it was it was a reference to Chinese customs. The previous Chinese governments were named after the old primitive states or geographic terms. Even Khitan and the Juchen. Khitan as well as the Juchen were following this custom by giving their states the names Liao (for Manchuria's Liao River within Manchuria) as well as Jin ("Gold," for the name of a river in Manchuria which had the Juchen name of that significance). Yuan is the first name that was not geographical in a Chinese tradition that has existed since Wang Mang built up the Xin line (AD 9-25).

In the 1260s, the central organization and the adjacent organisation in the Chinese domain were remodeled according to Chinese patterns, with specific changes made through China's Jin state. Its Central Secretariat remained the most prominently known authority for military personnel and had specific offices, such as the six traditional funds, the war officials, ceremonies, discipline and open work. In addition, the Shumiyuan (Military Council) was a different establishment that was acquired by previous administrations. The Yushitai (Censorate) had been originally created to fight the ruler and to study strategies, but eventually it became a tool of the court itself as well as an instrument to eliminate other members of the group. In the beginning, the regional divisions resembled Chinese models, but the freedom of the local area was not as high as it was during the Song and the common organisations were part of the Central Secretariat. The structure of the various regular organizations across China were merely a re-creation that of that of Central Secretariat. According to Chinese sources, during 1260-61 the lower echelons of the Central Secretariat were for the majority Chinese and the top workplaces however and regardless of whether they had traditional Chinese name, was reserved for non-Chinese. It is shocking that Kublai Khan had not many Mongols in top regulatory positions and was sceptical of some of his ancestors and favored the outright intruders. In the military, the circle of influence was not influenced by efforts to achieve an amalgamation of Chinese and local customs and the Mongol privilege remained dominant.

There were a lot of partisan ethnic and social gatherings took place within the Yuan government to ensure that there was a consistent regular. The traditional Chinese worth system had disappear to a large extent and no morality of the political sphere could have replaced it. While the customary dependability centered on the leader, the friendship of nokor relationships was not enough to bind the diverse decisions into a coherent unit. The skewed arrangement of the government might work under an able ruler, but with a weak or incompetent head, there was a risk of crumbling and a drop in productivity was a result.

The former researchers in China remain, as they was, out of the regulatory and legislative structure and only minor posts were accessible to them. The Mongols didn't use the authoritative capabilities of the researchers they feared their capabilities and abilities. The decision to leave the majority of China was more of a top-of-the-line of colonialists rather than an element that was part of Chinese social structure.

The inability from the Mongols to integrate their culture with Chinese is evident in their attempts to consolidate the weaknesses of their traditional. After the Song realm was destroyed and the population in China was divided in four groups. They were the Mongols who were a small but popular minority. The next group was semuren ("people who have a status of extraordinary") which were members of confederations with the Mongols such as Turks as well as Middle Eastern Muslims. The third group was referred to as the "hanren" (a term that for majority of the time implies Chinese however it was used to identify the inhabitants of only north China) The group included Chinese and other ethnic communities that were part of the former Jin state, such in they were Xi Xia, Juchen, Khitan, Koreans, Bohai, and Tangut and could be employed in various capacities and were also the governing body of the military forces that were under Mongol administration. The final gathering was known as the manzi or Manzi the pejorative term in Chinese meaning "southern brute,"" which was the name given to the previous people from Song China (around three-fourths of the Chinese domain). The lowest layer of Yuan China was involved by the slaves, whose number was huge. The status of slaves was genetic and only under certain conditions could a person be released.

Over four-fifths of people in the country were part of the nanren group that was often barred from higher positions (just rarely would any of them be elevated to the level of a certain quality). The Mongols and semuren were not subject to charges and enjoyed the safety of law more than the hanren or the nanren.

The standard distinction between various ethnic groups and their comparing status was not an Mongol change, but rather a separation of the social obtained through Jin. Jin state. In the same way, many establishments were acquired from Jin. Laws in Yuan China was largely based on the law of Jin and in a limited way on the conventional Chinese law. Mongol legitimate organizations and practices also performed an amazing task, especially when it came to reforming law. The Yuan legal code was preserved in the dynastic past, Yuanshi, just as various sources. Additionally, a variety of rules, laws, and the judicial decisions of individual cases are collected in gatherings like, Yuandianzhang, which toss the light on the legal framework and social norms once all is said and completed.

Mongol along with Chinese dualism are also evident in management documents and the dialects. The majority of the decisions Mongols even during the last long period of the Yuan were conversant in Chinese as well, and the percentage who could master in the Chinese content was small. In reality, only two Chinese attempted to get acquainted with the dialects of their respective winners. The local and organizational system therefore had to rely to a large degree on interpreters and mediators. Mongol was the primary language used for all decisions or pronouncements, as well as mandates were originally written in Mongol and an adaptation of a Chinese interlinear format was added. The Chinese adaptation was written in the informal style rather than the traditional narrative style, and was in line with an informal style of writing. It was based on the Mongol word request, with the intention that it is more likely than not as sexy to local elite. Many of the Chinese adaptations are available to a variety of sources, such as, Yuandianzhang.

Economy

It was the Mongol triumph of Song domain came about because, since the end of the Tang it reunified the entire of China. Melody China was able to exchange with its neighboring countries, the Liao and Jin however, the exchange was carefully monitored and restricted to market outskirts. The Mongol victory later brought China back into the economy. The Mongol organisation determined to utilize the wealth of the former Song domain, which was the most prosperous part of China and attempted to move forward in exchange, and aimed at greater coordination between the north and south. The capital's area was dependent on the transport of grain from south, and huge quantities of materials and nourishment were needed to sustain in the Mongol armies. It was the Grand Canal, which had linked the frameworks of the Yangtze and the Huai and the Huang in the late seventh century, was constructed and extended out to Dadu between 1292 and 1293 through the use in corvee (unpaid work) under the direction of a well-known Chinese stargazer and designer driven by pressure Guo Shoujing. This was a completely different activity within Chinese customs. It was then retracted the year 1292, however with another step in the area of financial correspondences, which was considered to be unusual to Chinese eyes. Around 1280, concessions to grain transport outside of China were given to private Chinese businessmen in the southeastern area of the beachfront (some Chinese government authorities were generally hostile towards ventures and private exchange and ventures, a Chinese Mongols didn't agree with). Private shipowners moved their armadas grains out of the Lower Yangtze district to the northern Chinese harbors, and then from that point to the capital city. In the early years of the 14th century, however the owners of private armadas who had made huge fortunes, were accused of inequity and robbery and the whole activity was stopped. The Mongol government was never able to replace the armadas of the government.

Another aspect that contributed to the flourishing exchange in China was the normalization of money. It was the case that Song and Jin were the first to offer paper cash but only in conjunction with bronze coins, which maintained the lawful principal. It was the Yuan administration was first in the world to establish paper cash as the primary legal money across the world (1260). This encouraged exchanges involving money in the private sector similar to those in government treasuries. In the time the economy was positive, the dependence on money in the form of paper as main source of currency had no negative impact on the economy. The moment the economy began to decline under the previous Mongol ruler, the paper money became worthless and the expansion began. One reason behind the paper money could have been that lots of copper and bronze was used to support the Buddhist group and its sculptures as well as another reason that metal minerals that China sufficient to provide enough coins for more than 80 million people.

A strict and rigorous life

The Mongols didn't try to force their faith (a part known as paradise), the forces of nature and shamanistic beliefs) on their subjects. This was akin to the existing religions in China and China, which included what Mongol rulers believed was"sanjiao" ("three lesson") Daoism, Buddhism and Confucianism. Each of Daoism and Buddhism were distinct in their character and associations, and even though they were often equal to each other but they weren't completely separate. The Neo-Confucianism cult of the Zhu Xi school delighted in normal status following the 1310s. However, the followers of the three schools were connected both mentally and logically in a way that facilitated their "amalgamation" of three schools in people of the common man and elite, and even the people living in remote areas of China.

Daoism

In the Jin administration, some prominent Daoist groups were flourishing in the northern part of China and Genghis Khan was enthralled by Changchun, the Daoist leader Changchun. In 1223, Genghis Khan permitted Changchun as well as his followers to be exempted from all charges and obligations demanded by the administration. This was the first in an escalating series of proclamations that granted special advantages to the ministries of the various religions of China.

It seemed as if Daoism from China would be able to gain favour among the Mongol rulers, to the detriment to Chinese Buddhism. However, the Buddhists also benefited from the open-mindedness of the court. They tried to establish a foothold within the family of the supreme, triggered by the fact that many Buddhist establishments were influenced with the Daoists who relied on Mongol generosity. In the reign of the great Khan Mongke some talks were conducted in between Daoist as well as the Buddhist ministries (1255-58) and ended with an agreement that the old Buddhist sanctuary should be reverted the reason for which they were originally created. Magnificent demands also prohibited some imaginative Daoist writings, which claimed that Buddhism was presented as part of Daoism as well as the Buddha as an incarnation of Laozi who was the creator of Daoism. In reality, Daoism as such kept its existence under the Yuan and the financial benefits originally granted to the Daoist followers of Changchun were made available on an equal basis to all religious institutions.

Buddhism

The followers from Chinese Buddhism under the early Mongol rulers were part of the Chan (Zen) faction (a concentration upon contemplation). Their sophisticated and high-intelligence aesthetics, however they didn't enthralle the Mongols who were attracted by the mix of enchantment exercises, but not formless mysticism, and awe-inspiring images in the visual arts associated with Tibetan Buddhism. Kublai Khan named a youthful Tibetan lama who was known under the name of 'Phags-dad' as a dazzling preceptor (dishi) who morphed into the chief of the Buddhist faith throughout every Mongol region, which included China. A strange government organisation was created in 1264 in order to administer Buddhism and function as a sort of department of the amazing preceptor. It was in charge of Buddhist questions when all is declared to be done as well as Tibetan issues, even though Tibet was not part of the organisation of China legitimate and the existence of no Mongol battalions were ever established in Tibet. Tibetan officials from the government had been successful in this manner on the Mongol court, and also in achieving an apparent autonomy.

Following the triumph of Song China after the victory of Song China, an amazing office to oversee Buddhism within southern China was created and was heavily influenced an additional Tibetan lama. The result was two supervisory Buddhist offices: one located in Dadu to oversee northwestern China in northern China and Tibet and the other in Lin'an for the southern part of China. The southern office created a huge amount of discontent among Chinese Buddhists as well as the general public everywhere due to its brutal and violent methods, property seizures and blackmailing from the masses. Through the Yuan tradition, complaints were raised against the self-important behavior and conduct of Tibetan lamas. (Under the previous Togon-temur, the ruler, Tibetan ministers acquainted the court with customs of sexuality calling for the sanctification of females to have a sexual relationship. These rituals were are not new to Indian as well as Tibetan societies, but quite shocking to the Chinese high-end.)

While Buddhism had achieved a victory in the ruling minority of China but it was outside rather than Chinese Buddhism. The popular varieties of Buddhism especially Chan Buddhism, kept on operating, and cloisters in the southern part of China at times transformed into a secluded area of normal human progress , where lay and priests Buddhists were able to develop the same paintings, verse and all the academic related interests of the Chinese elite class of literati however they may, in the end, Chinese Buddhism was a part of the overall conditions of China's Yuan domain. The exemption from corvee and fees attracted thousands of people to live a holy life to fulfill their needs; as society degraded more people looked to seek refuge behind the walls of the community that separated the religious. Around 1300 , the number of priests throughout China was estimated at 500,000, and was is more likely than not that it was developed in the latest years of Mongol guidelines. Priests performed a remarkable role during the uprisings, which the Yuan domain, in the long end was defeated; also the first Ming sovereign was priest for a long period of time.

Remote religions

Tibetan Buddhism consistently stayed outside Chinese development, and so did other religions that were imported. A certain number of Muslims arrived in China and were all of them from in the Middle East or from Central Asia. It is believed that the Turkic Ongut clan is,, to the greatest extent Nestorian Christian. Numerous headstones featuring an inscription that is dual Turkic and Chinese engraving have been protected but none of the devotees is believed to be Chinese according to the source. An census taken around 1500 in Zhenjiang (in the current area of Jiangsu) documents the Nestorians as well as other nationalities. The number of Nestorian Christians in China was exorbitant to the extent that in 1289, an organization specifically to oversee them was set in Dadu. Manichaeism was a religion that had been introduced into China in the Tang and was eradicated as a religious system that was dispersed under the Yuan but some Manichaean people were likely to be sucked into messianic Buddhist groups, such as The White Lotus order, a gathering that attracted many followers from those in the Chinese less privileged.

Confucianism

Confucianism was considered in the eyes of Mongols as an Chinese religionand was a mix of fortunes in their traditional. The teachings that were taught by Confucianism from the Neo-Confucian schools that was founded by Zhu Xi from the Song period were familiar to the Mongol court in Zhongdu in the 1230s, but were only available to restricted circles in Zhongdu and in the northern part of China. Confucian researchers recognized the advantages that were extended to the ministry, all things being equal, however they were dealt a serious hit when the scholarly assessments were canceled following the Mongol victory. For a long time , the tests, based on Confucian writings, were the main reason behind the selection of officials and their privileged status within the society and in the state. Following Kublai's rise

Confucianism experienced an increasing passionate gathering within the Mongol court due to the efforts of Chinese counsellors like, Liu Bingzhong and the legendary Confucian Ace Xu Heng. Under their direction the Mongol court, a particular Confucianization took place in government and in instruction. Chinese ceremonies were held for a while in the sanctuary of the dynastic dynasty (taimiao) that was established in Zhongdu in the year 1263. State sacrifices were offered to Confucius and the study in the Classics was backed. In any event there was a significant number of the ceremonies performed in the court were at least Tibetan Buddhist or acquired from the Mongol itinerant past, were followed. King Buyantu (ruled 1311 - 20) One of the most sinicized Mongol rulers, reinstated the framework of assessment in 1313. However, it remains unclear how the tests performed. They did not guarantee the vocation of an official, like the ones under Song and, in a way more recently, under Jin had done.

The structure of the Yuan that was presented in 1313, offered different kinds of education plans to Mongols as well as other outsiders (semuren) and Chinese Additionally the requirements were exceptional: Chinese needed to show their complete dominance over the education program, while Mongols as well as other outsiders were required to show a mediocre display. This disparity was also officially recognized for those newcomers who were admitted to the foundation of the state (guozijian). The main assessments were conducted in the presence of the sovereign at 1315 and among the 300 people who were given an official title such as specialist (jinshi) 75 were Mongols and 75 were outsiders and 75 were Northern Chinese (hanren) as well as 75 were from southern China and all were granted official status within the administration, with Mongols being the top posts, and Chinese the lower positions. The positions of power within the hierarchy of command remained at the disposal of the Mongols and other outsiders.

In Buyantu, it was because the editorials and translations that were part of the Neo-Confucian School became obligatory. This consolidated the Neo-Confucian faith system, not only for the Chinese elite who wanted to complete an examination but as well for those in the future. Chinese Confucian universality from the fourteenth century to the nineteenth century was based heavily on the established institutions it been granted during the Yuan. In spite of this, Classical grants under the Yuan did not produce a single magnificent work but was nonetheless fought against an adversarial political and academic context. In an effort to safeguard their sacred custom as well as their consecrated convention Confucian scholars were satisfied clarifying the precepts formulated in the Song savants. They tried to organize the various philosophical perspectives and issues rather than focusing on the development of new avenues of inquiry.

Writing

Chinese writing from the time also showed moderate tendencies. Verse was a popular distraction for the educated class, which included the Sinicized scholars of Mongol, Central Asian, and western Asian birthplaces. However, not a lot of extraordinary work or advances were made. The last riotous times of Yuan, many eminent artists emerged, such as the mutable Yang Weizhen and the strong and erratic Gao Qi. Many compositions dealing with current events and individuals were written under the Yuan However, they stand out for their substance and not for their academic legitimacy. A shockingly harsh analysis and parody of the Mongols and unveiled Song support was discovered in the openness of articulation, likely due to the fact that the Mongols were not interested in what Chinese were writing in Chinese and were, for the most part, not able to comprehend the language. Some authors collected unusual interesting and fascinating things and shared a lot that comprise Song culture to those who would come in the future. They grieve for the perfection and splendor of the Song. Song is a constant theme in Yuan's writings.

In the middle of the Yuan time period during the Yuan time frame, the standard Chinese authoritative historiography of the time was revived under the direction of the Hanlin Academy, which supported the collection of the authoritative dynastic histories from those of the Song, Liao, and Jin states that were defeated to the Mongols and attempted to create an assemblage of the annals for rule (shilu) as well as other abstracts of administrative records. The most significant achievement of true historiography was the collection (1329-33) of Jingshi dadian which was an archive comprising 800 Juan (sections) of legal law and records; however, the information is now lost. Private historiography specifically is a look during the times of the Song which was a shaky performance under the Yuan because of the hostile political and academic climate. The most well-known commitment was written by Ma Duanlin and titled Wenxian tongkao ("General Study of the Literary Remains") A comprehensive story of Chinese organizations from the earliest time to the time of the central government that was Nan Songline. Nan Songline.

In urban cultures, writing in the language of the vernacular was gaining momentum, and not restricted by rigid standards of formalist or universalist ideology. The creation of stories and books was to keep the wide-ranging openness of emotional writing was at an unbeatable level the Yuan China and later, abstract analysis saw as the Yuan as the standard age for operatic arias also known as qu (a word that is also used for a full play which includes arias as well as recited the recitatives). The selection Yuanquxuan ("Selection of Yuan Operas"), that includes 100 show lyrics and the narrator's "brief books" to record sensationalized sentiments like Sanguo ("Three kingdoms") offer ample proof of the inventiveness and importance that is Chinese emotion-driven writing. This treasure could be seen as proof that under Yuan specific urbanization took place and the concept of a bourgeoisie was born due to the sensational writing and informal books found their majority between the craft and vendor classes.

Outsiders, mostly from Turkic or Persian origin, also contributed the Chinese composition under Yuan. They wrote verses and painted along the Chinese path to distinguish themselves from the fields in which they could discern distinction from the educated Chinese. The outsiders that wrote their works in Chinese seem to have shied away from any references to their distant source or the doctrine they adhered to. Absolutely nothing, if truth be told can be any more Chinese than their works. Even foreigners who, as with the Persians were a nation that had an amazing artistic tradition that was its own, never attempted to show their local culture, structures or religious beliefs. There was no abstract beneficial interaction to be feasible even though China was exposed to more outside influences during the Yuan than at any other period in recent history, Chinese writing shows little influence from these interactions with the world outside. Perhaps it is a sign of the times that during the Yuan there were no abstract works of various civic institutions were rewritten to Chinese and no interpretations that reinterpreted Chinese Classical and authentic works to Mongol remain. It appeared that it was just the choice of a complete disdain for Chinese development, as taught by the majority of Mongols or ignoring the repercussions of Chinese cultural.

Human experience expressed through expressions

Conservatism played a prominent role in the human expressions of the Mongol period. In the case of supported expressions, such as like pottery and figure and figure, the Mongols are enticed to make an argument for the Chinese amazing legacy was not supported by any profound idea of their own conservatism was a an easy propagation. Tune, Liao, and Jin clay types were reintroduced in a manner that was often unique, shaped by an expanded mass. The incredible masterful achievement of the time, the blue and white item, was likely to come from non-superior sources. The state-sponsored Buddhist model frequently reached high levels of imaginative standards that protected the authenticity and incredible articulated that was characteristic of Tang and Song practices, and in the greatest model of the period like the reliefs found at Juyong Pass north of Dadu (1342-45) This was coupled with a vibrant aesthetic theme on the surface and an enthralling sensation that was more suited to the outside world than the distinctly restricted Chinese elegant.

Conservatism also weakened the calligraphy and painting arts as a private art and painting. The beginners who created their work felt the need to safeguard their work from an apparent dangerous threat. Conservatism, however, often was seen as a creative restoration that scoured the past for sources of inspiration and then imaginatively transformed them into a different form of speech. Calligraphy was one of the most popular styles. Zhao Mengfu gave a fresh impetus to the fourth century fashion that was developed by Wang Xizhi, which at the time became an established common style for

Chinese composition and printing books for a significant amount of time. When it came to painting Zhao along with his rival Qian Xuan assisted with finishing the development of a distinctive basic style that established a phase throughout the history in Chinese composition. Their work was not a continuation of the tradition of the past however, it was broadly based on the common past convention and the styles of the past in contrast to observed objects, became the object of imagination. Naturalism in Song painting gave way to calligraphicly roused reflections. Artistic creations were found to be strongly linked to the meticulous engravings which appeared on them with an increasing recurrence, and a distinct quality. Professionally-designed systems that were efficient and with evident visual appeal were kept off, replaced by deliberate clumsiness and an intellectualized boost. The works of these artists were created for private use, usually documenting or obscuring personal and political thoughts, that could be appreciated by literati who were merely interested in the simple implications of their subject and expressive references or engravings.

The naturalistic styles of art were also gaining popularity all through the beginning six-month time and was painted by such notable experts like Li Kan, and Ren Renfa. Incorporating northern traditions of during the Tang and Song times These styles were practiced mostly by researchers who were connected to the court in the capital. Certain members of the Mongol royal family became major supporters or leaders of these conservatism, but their support was not as strong in comparison with the previous times.

In the third quarter of the traditional period, which saw an abrupt decrease in the practice of painting by researchers and northerners, Yuan painting was progressively discussed by the imaginative method of Zhao Mengfu, as practiced with antisocial scholars from the territory of Suzhou-Wuxing. Four of them -- the painting of scenes Huang Gongwang, Wu Zhen, Ni Zan, and Wang Meng--alternated and merged certain elements of the past into very close to home distinct styles that eventually came to be recognized as"the" Four Masters of the Yuan administration. At the beginning of Ming period the Hongwu head destroyed the Suzhou literary world and the Suzhou painting. Before the 15th century, regardless, Suzhou craftsmen by and were controlled Chinese canvas and the styles that were exhibited by The Four Masters turned into the most captivating of all works of art models later in Chinese time.

Chapter 5: The Yassa

Temujin was a distinct kind of leader. Perhaps it was his conviction in a fairer management style that gave him the most authority. Temujin didn't believe in the concept of family-based appointment. Instead, he offered ranking based on skill and loyalty. Jelme as well as Boorchu had been his loyal servants for more than 10 years and were deserving to be promoted to a higher post. Temujin did make it to the Khan level, which was under Ong Khan, and ruled the tribe he was a part of. Even though it was a small tribe it was his reward for loyalty that helped attract his followers and soldiers.

One of the first appointments he held was with the cooks. He needed someone to trust in cooking his meals, butchering the meat and making sure that they were able to move huge cauldrons. For Temujin it was his first line of defense since his father was poisoned. He was not keen to go down exactly the same way due to clan rivals.

Archers were given roles. The archers of his were assigned to guard the herds and ensure that nobody tried to take them away and also his riches.

Kasar His large, strong brother, was appointed the responsibility of taking charge of the warriors. Kasar was the primary person responsible for protecting the game. Belgutei, a half-brother of Belgutei was responsible for their geldings and making sure the horses were near the main camp in the event that Temujin was required to move fast.

Temujin was afraid of being poisoned and was also terrified of being ambushed once more. He was in the process of training 150 elite bodyguards who would guard his camp, including 80 guards at night as well as 70 guards on daytime (Weatherford 2004).

While Temujin was gaining more fame and creating the best system of governance to his citizens, Jamuqa became his main opponent.

In the event that Genghis Khan was regarded as to be a bloodthirsty villain, then Jamuqa was surely right with Genghis Khan. Jamuqa was furious and used the excuse of an earlier raid by Temujin against him in order to fight his blood brother. Jamuqa was able to take down one of the chiefs of the attack. Jamuqa cut off the head of his victim and tied it to horse's tail, and then carried it across the steppes.

The horse's head was considered to be a sin against the family as was the horse's head, which was regarded since it was considered to be the most sacred portion within the body. There is also evidence that he seized 70 men from Khan's army and cooked them in cauldrons (Weatherford 2004). Of of course, the 70 men inside 70 cauldrons could be just a myth or the reality of what happened. It could be 7 people in seven cauldrons, however, as the story was told , it increased in numbers to make it even more terrifying and to increase the fame of Jamuqa.

It isn't clear if Yassa was the Mongol Empire, which was led by the Mongols was founded around the same timeframe as continuing battles and raids with Jamuqa. The code was created through decrees during time of war.

The Yassa is difficult to comprehend since it was a secret legal code that was written in a book. It was considered to be the actual code of law for the Empire however, it was always a secret code, with no public announcement.

Because Genghis Khan was a ferocious fighter during his teens as well as early 20s fighting and also establishing loyal followers, it is likely that many law he enforced were formulated in order to defeat his enemies. Then, when that the Mongol Empire was founded the decrees expanded to include the lifestyle and culture of.

Genghis Khan research suggests that he kept the rules and laws secret as these decrees were able to be changed or re-used if needed, instead of being in place always. If the Khan was satisfied, the decree could have been altered.

Khan will certainly seek something beneficial to him in the event that something becomes necessary. To rule his tribe it was required to take his brother's life, however earlier laws forbade such an act. The prospect of being an enslaved person for a short period of time is not going to have gone over well, which is why Khan may have kept the laws secret for the purpose of making sure that he could alter the laws whenever necessary.

Three Parts of the Yassa Three Parts of the Yassa

These laws of Yassa were created to keep their members, including soldiers, officers and doctors, steadfast. Genghis Khan was a strict leader, and the binding of clans of nomads and punishment for any wrongdoing. The laws were created for being for and by the masses, not property. Khan allowed a person to admit a mistake and would not issue an indictment of guilt.

Many of the decrees addressed social and economic conflicts. It was essential to have laws in place to maintain the Mongols loyal and also to make new friends. Some of the rules included:

* No livestock should be stolen.

* Food items must be shared among travelers

* Women are not able to be taken away from other families.

* Soldiers should not leave the country.

These four rules appear to be simple and it's evident why these laws were put in place. Khan didn't have many animals as an infant and it was tough to keep the things he owned. Khan's brother is known for his stealing as well as horde and was never one to offer help to his family, let alone strangers. Nobody else ever assisted Khan neither. The saga of Borte's arrest and abuse made it necessary to create regulations regarding women, so that nothing could happen to a man's wife as the way it was happening to Borte. He also wanted everyone to remain loyal to him and not be a slave to other rulers, or worse , deceive him, and any war plans he may have considered.

The punishment was not varied significantly. In the majority of cases, it would be death via beheading. Noble blood was protected from being killed, so that they did not spill any drop of their blood, but, they'd be executed. Small violations of the law were punishable with death. Soldiers could be executed if he didn't show normal courtesy to someone else. If, for instance, someone drops something by person, the person standing before him must be aware of it and then pick the item up.

Genghis Khan didn't murder easily, particularly when it was the people who were favoured by Genghis Khan. He was willing to give preference, and would give them many possibilities before punishment was handed out.

It is not something Khan attempted to control or exploit. Perhaps it was this law or the acceptance to his religion that's the most significant. Genghis Khan allowed people to practice religion with freedom. They could worship any god or Gods or religions they wanted, so long as they remained loyal to the Yassa code of conduct.

Certain laws are simply speculation because there is no evidence in writing. One of those laws dealt with declaring someone "emperor" without having to be elected. Officers, princes Khans, princes, and Mongol nobles who were part of the general council were required the right to select an individual as emperor. If this didn't happen and the person was not elected, they was executed.

The law may also have said the peace between a monarch and king was prohibited. This could include having peace with a prince, or anyone who did not adhere to the Yassa law.

In times of war, it is believed that Khan demanded an "ruling that divided the men" into distinct numbered groups, each headed by a member of a group like a prince general or noyan, to oversee the army. The army could include in the thousands, hundreds, tens or ten thousand and was maintained in that numbers. This was believed to offer Khan an easy means to build his army in the shortest time frame and to fight off the enemies.

It was prohibited to pillage any opponent in the absence of a directive to do this was given. The permission needed to be granted by the commander. If a soldier was allowed to pillage the battlefield, the soldier had the same right as an officer to keep what they discovered, provided that the share was given to the emperor.

There were some people who didn't go to the war. These men were required to work for the empire with no pay for a specific amount of time. This was a method to make every person and every man contribute to the purpose of uniting the Mongols even if they didn't fight in battle.

Khan also abolished slavery and servitude for his Mongol people. Khan would require any Mongol belonging to a clan of enemies in his army to join however, they were not able to be slaves. The fact was that slaves or servants didn't exist however Khan typically turned non-Mongols the status of servants or slaves. Anyone who was from China, Russia, India or a different country that wasn't Mongol is either a slave or a captive.

Adulterers were sentenced to death and without any evaluation of whether he was married or not. Khan believed strongly in being in love with another, but not engaging in adultery or taking from one another, as per the historical records.

Concubines' children were deemed legitimate and were given their part of the family heritage. The father was expected to leave the estate of the concubine, and the rules had to be followed.

The Yassa contained around 32 laws, as speculated by experts. It was adopted as component of the Mongol Empire, during and following Genghis Khan's demise. Nowadays, Mongolia still uses the term Yassa. Some of the laws are also regarded as a part of their culture and culture, to be honored in the same way as they were back then.

Chapter 6: The Defeat Of The Tatars

When Genghis Khan wasn't fighting Jamuqa to expand his territory or to unite Mongolia and Mongolians, he was engaged in other conflicts. Genghis Khan had to accumulate an impressive amount of power in order to take on Jamuqa and the clans that dominated Mongolia.

The year 1195 was the one when Genghis Khan was granted the opportunity to expand his power to levels that were higher than it was. With his allegiance with Ong Khan as well as the Kereyid the Kereyid, he'd begin one of his most intense battles.

The Jurched Kingdom was a major sticking spot for power. This Jurched Kingdom was located in the region to the south of Gobi. The kingdom was adept at keeping clans from being a part of it by forming alliances. They employed tactics to stop smaller clans from fighting each other. This ensured that the tribes remained fragile and they would not attempt to compete with against Jurched people to gain the power.

Genghis Khan was striving to increase his strength and army. Many historians believe that Genghis Khan had only 20,000 soldiers of his army at the time of his first battles. It was only after the battle against Tatars Tatars that he started to accumulate an number of warriors in his army, which was 100,000. Genghis Khan was in his 30s at the time of his conquest, and began to earn respect from his peers, and also for the shrewdness demonstrated in his battle against other tribes.

It was the first battle between the Tatar. The war began to rage in 1195, however the battle didn't occur until 1196.

The Jurched ruler, known as the Golden Khan, began to initiate Ong Khan to rebel with the Tatars. The kingdom was initially associated with the Tatar but they went on to grow in the power of Tatars. This is definitely not what The Golden Khan would want. It could be the end of his kingdom, should it was allowed to be ruled by the Tatars take over the kingdom.

It wasn't that the Jurched Kingdom felt more favorably towards Temujin. Rather, their concern was in the event that the Tatar was likely to prevail in a straight fight. Ong Khan asked Temujin's assistance to aid in the fight.

It was winter in 1196. Ong Khan as well as Temujin began to set off with their troops to battle the Tatar. The idea was to attack similar to the way they did in the steppes of Mongolia. But, with more soldiers on the battlefield, victory was simple.

Early Raid Tactics

The Mongols were nomadic and that made them more robust than the other people. The Mongols were able to survive on the land even in the most extreme of circumstances. They didn't need to worry about hunger or deprivation of food since they were on the move together with herds.

They also had three to four horses each soldier. With spare horses, they could ride for hours without stopping. When one horse became tired of carrying a person, they would change horses and continue riding. Horses were also used that were more mobile for those fighting the Mongol forces. The breed of horse was very tough, also. It is possible that they were smaller than certain breeds however they could withstand the harsh desert, cold, and the other severe conditions that could cause death to other breeds.

Different cultures were dependent on their apparatus and heavy armor however Khan's nomad soldiers. Khan was able to bring individuals of his soldiers as scouts to find better ways and better terrain for fighting. Khan was not afraid to take chances, especially when the route was clearly traced. Genghis Khan made his soldiers to be trained in archery, horsemanship and tactics for the unit. Rotations and formations were practiced every time they weren't fighting. Training was intended to be tough however it was not overly demanding.

Mongols Mongols could stay clear of any micromanagement in the army since they let the leaders and their subordinates. When the goal was achieved they were able to discover weaknesses and to consider their own ideas. If it was deemed to be the best method of completing the mission the order was followed. The loyalty of each other and also to the superiors was established to ensure that nobody fled the battlefield, or turn against the Khan.

Six out of all soldiers were archers. The rest would have lances. The Khan advocated lighter armor and could perform military executions that which other armies couldn't manage. They had head gear that protected them as well as body armor, however, it wasn't like knights from Europe.

Sheer Numbers

The battle against the Tatar was all about numbers. The tactics employed by the military to combat smaller clans were employed against the Tatars however, due to Ong Khan coming into the battle and Ong Khan joining the fight, the Tatars were not able to prevail. It was especially challenging because that the Jurched Kingdom in alliance together with Ong Khan. Lack of assistance for Tatars left them vulnerable.

There was nothing to hide an army advancing towards another clan in the Steppes. This was an open area and the Tatar didn't have a large fortification that kept Genghis Khan from the area, just as in the Jurched Kingdom.

The victory was significant not just in the way it was carried out however, but in the prize that was awarded in exchange for beating the Tatar. Tatars Tatar trade with China in exchange for some of the finest products like pearls, silk and other riches. Genghis Khan was able to hold the wealth they stole away from Tatars. Silk clothing was better that any Mongol followers or even he ever before had.

The goods that were traded have had a profound influence on Khan. It was an opportunity which brought doors open since the Tatar had relations to China and Jurched which he could make use of. The Tatar also demonstrated to his supporters that they weren't right to be loyal to the Tatar. Anyone who could earn the kind of wealth he did must be a person worth following.

Genghis Khan was studying with Genghis Khan was learning from Jurched people. He could tell by their constant re-alliances there was no guarantee of permanence. There was never a time when a fight was really over until one was able to gain total commitment from all. Changes of the association could lead to an entirely new battle or shift in attitude could be the result. Genghis Khan was in need of a way to make his clanand his rule more effective and also the best option for the many whom he defeated.

This ability transformed him into a leader. It wasn't enough to fight battles, won and formed alliances. He needed to be a figure to follow. What followed was the desire of Temujin to be his Jurched Kingdom.

Jurched, the Kingdom Jurched was richer than the Tatar because of their numerous trade choices. It was the Golden Khan also had numerous clans who were willing to support him.

The Wealth of the Wealthy to start an Empire

Khan's position in the world was strengthened due to the wealth he accumulated by acquiring the Tatar. This was enough money that he could expand into new areas, including those with a direct lineage. He was always thought to be lower in certain clans because of his bloodline, but it was becoming less of a really matter to certain. To others, it was a major concern that an insurgent was growing and becoming more powerful.

Chapter 7: Jurkin Betrayal And Khan's Message

The Jurkin clan was part of his family tree. They were distant family members. He requested a reunion with Jurkin Jurkin in advance of the battle against the Tatars. At first , the Jurkins were in agreement. He arranged together to get them together, so that they could leave for battle with the Tatar. Temujin was waiting for six days however, the Jurkin did not show up.

Although they had promised to help initially however, the Jurkin didn't have any feelings of loyalty to Temujin. Their absence was a vote in his favor. This was similar to the khuriltai where only a handful of people showed up in support of Temujin, while the majority members of the elite khans didn't think it was important to stand behind Temujin. The Jurkins were not confident in Temujin's abilities to prevail in the fight.

The meal was not one you can be proud about. The half-brother of Temujin was snubbed by the Jurkin attempted to get the horse. Buri the Wrestler entered the fight, and cut the half-brother's shoulder, drawing a small amount of blood, and the whole feast was thrown into a brawl. It was because of the indifference to Temujin's that allowed the snark to prevail. But, Temujin received the assurance that the Jurkin tribe would be fighting the Tartar. With such a wealthy and powerful tribe, Temujin was not be concerned about the fact that the Jurkins won't be able to claim some of the spoils from the raid.

However, the Jurkin had other ideas. According to the Secret History and Weatherford, both acknowledge that the Jurkins considered it a good idea to go after Khan's camp in the midst of they were on their way to battle the Tatar.

The Jurkin was absent. Jurkin killed 10 Temujin's followers and stripped them of all their belongings as well as clothes. This was not the best choice to take. Temujin had suffered a lot in his youth and was able to form strong alliances with his soldiers. His treatment of his followers was so exceptional compared against other leaders they were certain that the Khan was the one to follow.

Revenge from Wealth

Temujin increased his territory and wealth with the victory over the Tatars. The year 1197 was the time that Temujin had a plan to take revenge on the Jurkin. The Jurkin were not given an opportunity against the warriors of Temujin. Their strength and discipline swiftly defeated the Jurkin during the battle taking them down, giving Temujin the opportunity to set an example for others who would oppose his.

In addition, the victory was significant for soothing the anger of his enemies, displaying his strength, and demonstrating the strength of his warriors and strength, but it was also the time the Yassa rules were first created. his own Yassa rules. He offered loyal allies and warriors positions following the tradition that family members had. The rewards of a skill became recognized. The word spread that the Khan did not intend to be solely focused on the bloodline you came from but rather on the abilities as well as your intelligence and above all, your loyalty to him.

Temujin's New Policy

It is evident that Temujin was an example to follow more than just making appointments for his warriors. He also needed to display his power in different ways. Nobody was willing to honor him because they believed that bloodline and lineage were important. The Jurkin had proven that they were not, and Temujin went beyond just looting the camp and taking the spoils from war. He went further than the idea of enslavement, leaving participants of the Jurkins to organize and attack later .

The khuriltai was requested by the man the council of speciality, to convene. He wanted to hold a public trial of the aristocratic rulers. He was seeking justice not only on the battlefield but from all the powerful leaders. He demanded that to see the Jurkin to be held accountable for their actions in breaking their pledge to assist him smuggle the Tatar and end their power. end.

The Jurkin leadership were found to be guilty. He ordered them to be executed. The executions were a powerful assertion, "You, who are noble blood, are not immune from the wrath of God." There is no special treatment for nobles of any lineage.

Temujin took over the Jurkin property, occupying it and dispersing people from the Jurkin clan to his family's homes but in no way as slaves. Temujin demonstrated to his clans and other members that Jurkin who were absorbed into their tribe were treated with respect and not treated as slaves. He even adopted an orphan of Jurkin's family Jurkin clan, gifted the child to his mother to care for, and then accepted the Jurkin clan members as his brothers in arms.

It wasn't the first time he'd admitted orphans. If one thinks about how Temujin was considered a child who was not the support of a father, one will feel his sentiments towards children who were not surrounded by family. He adopted a child in one of the Merkit, Tayichiud and Tatar tribes following their defeat. These adoptions were definitely politically motivated, but they were probably also sentimental and emotional.

By allowing orphans to be adopted by bringing them in, he demonstrated his willingness admit clan members from tribes that were defeated. He demonstrated that they could be equally involved with the newly conquered tribes as well as the prosperity his clan was earning.

Buri the Wrestler

Buri was guilty of an unforgivable crime against Khan's brother Belgutei. Temujin hosted a meal and advised Belgutei and Buri to fight. Buri was a champion wrestler, according to legend. Being aware of what had happened to his clan's leaders , and bewildered by Temujin's presence, Buri let Belgutei throw his body.

The match was traditionally thought to have ended. Buri was defeated, and it was possible to have Belgutei's honour restored. However, Temujin did not seem to think so. Belgutei grabbed Buri at the shoulder, put an elbow in the back of Bur's and shattered the spinal cord. Buri was then taken away, leaving him to be killed.

Temujin had given Belgutei the command to take down the man. Buri is also believed to be the final member of the Jurkin Temujin had to get rid of the planet. The final outcome of his vengeance and ultimate plot against Jurkin sent a clear message.

Anybody who disloyal to him or who lied to him will die on the steppes, regardless of whether they were nobles or relatives. If the defeated sided with the defeated, they would receive more respect and rewards to show their loyalty.

The Kherlen

In Mongolia the land, which was known as Avarga was used as the base camp of Temujin. At the time, it was an isolated camp that Temujin shared with Kherlen tribe members. Kherlen tribe. However, it soon was more important for him as an important base. Avarga was considered to be the ideal habitat for herders due to the presence of the sun's light and warmth that the sun provides. There was an entrance point that protected the cold winds from the north and plenty of water from the river and near Temujin's birthplace.

Jamuqa's Latest Attempt

After the battle and the defeat that of Jurkin it became apparent to Jamuqa Ong Khan as well as Temujin had a chance which had to be defeated. He was required to eliminate the rival clan which was clearly competing for the loyalty of all of Mongolia.

Before beginning any combat, Jamuqa decided to call on the khuriltai. He wanted to declare that he was Gur-khan the head over all the chiefs. His followers pledged loyalty.

Actually, it was an all-new swear of loyalty that was requested by him when he received his title as chief among chiefs.

Jamuqa was not a fan of his title, but the anger it could cause in other people. One method of showing disrespect was to obtain titles that were legally the property of someone else. Ong Khan's uncle was the holder of the title Gur-khan. But Ong Khan's uncle was killed when his fellow Kereyid community and Ong Khan were at war. Ong Khan killed the uncle of his, and nobody had taken the title Gur-khan ever since. Jamuqa was a public opponent to Ong Khan and Temujin's power.

Even though the title was awarded but it does not mean Jamuqa had won the whole issue of bringing Mongolia under one head. Temujin's followers were large however, the Gur-khan would need to win the war against Temujin to effectively assume the position as the chief among all Chiefs.

The fear of being feared as a military tactic

How would you react if were facing a formidable force? What would happen in the event that you had to face the bear? Your first instinct would be to get away from those enormous jaws that break bone. It's not a good idea to fight. If you are running, the bear is typically more likely to take your life, but not when you take your stand and appear less intimidating.

Temujin's primary purpose was making his foe afraid enough to leave the scene if they saw him fighting and standing. There were a variety of tactics used to terrorize the forces in opposition.

The Spirit Banners intended to symbolize God's and the belief of the ancients in the one over the other and were employed.

* Shamans who played drums as well as ritual equipment were also employed.

Temujin And Ong Khan were a huge number of warriors. The two had more fighters than Jamuqa and Ong Khan, which was certainly beneficial in provoking fear in the enemies' eyes.

But, it was also the psychological benefit that Temujin had. The shamans on his list were so extensive that the warriors of Jamuqa's clan became scared. They couldn't believe that they had a chance to win in the face of such a huge amount of "spiritual" strength in the hands of Temujin.

In the epic battle, Jamuqa aligned with Tayichiud. They Tayichiud were now Temujin's foes. The Tayichiud were responsible for the capture of Temujin's father in his youth. Because they were also aligned against the adversaries, this was extremely important to take them out.

It was not as simple as Temujin wanted. Yes, there was some fear but the Tayichiud did not have a shortage of numbers to beat. Temujin and Tayichiud engaged in a fierce battle for the whole day by throwing rocks and arrows at one another. Temujin was slightly injured in his neck and lost consciousness by the evening. The evidence suggests that he woke up in the morning asking for mare's milk, but Jelme, his faithful follower, didn't have any. Jelme knew where to get it but it was inside the camp of the enemy.

Jelme moved through his own camp and that of the enemy in search of the milk, but even though there was no sign of it, one thing was certain. He was committed. He wore a bare-faced and naked humiliation to receive the help his leader required to be healed. If this really happened or was just part of the mythology, it definitely showed how much Khan was a source of inspiration for his people.

Another great thing that occurred in the night. Nobody knew that Temujin was injured by the clan of Tayichiud. Many fled in fear it would be the end of their fight, and result in a loss. It was simple to take out those left.

Temujin was a role model similar to what he had set in the case of Jurkin. The leader was killed in order to ensure that they wouldn't rise up against his leadership. He offered a spot within his clan to those who were willing to accept his leadership and clan. For those who helped him escape his captivity, he released the slaves and welcomed as members of his clan.

Chapter 8: Tatar Defeated Twice

Following the defeat of Tayichiud, Jamuqa needed to regroup. It wasn't just their clan to give the strength needed by Genghis Khan's most formidable foe However, it was a major defeat for Genghis Khan. It was the year 1202. It was time to confront the remaining Tatar who had fled and still controlled a large portion of Mongolia. Ong Khan was beginning to get older and with couple of Merkit remaining strong He decided to stay close to home. He sent Temujin into battle with the Tatars and he travelled to the battleground and fought his remaining Merkit.

The second battle against the Tatars resulted in another alteration to the code, which the Temujin ruling was affirmed. Another change could be a source of anger for the aristocrats however it also benefited the people. This was the right choice. The strength, Genghis Khan had learned , came by getting "loved" to the masses as a leader, not the Aristocrats. It wasn't the tiny number of aristocrats to be fighting on the steppes however, it was the ordinary people.

After the his raid, he fought the remaining Tatars however, his attempt to steal the gers' treasures could not prevent him from complete victory. The strategy of launching an attack, chasing the defeated warriors, then leaving the camp to loot allowed the defeated warriors to retreat, recuperate their losses, and prepare for another attack. Temujin stated that looting was going to have to wait until Tatars were defeated completely.

Temujin left some individuals in the camp empty to make sure that nobody would be able to take the wealth before it was shared equally among the men. He captured the majority of warriors, fought off the warriors who were defeated and then eliminated them. Returning to the merchandise He was able to gain more control over the distribution.

He also set his troops to establish a new rule for widows and orphans from the dead warriors. For every person killed and who was an infant or widow who were widowed or children, they would be given part of the riches. It was discovered that the surviving family members who died in war would be cared for and not feared or even enslaved.

It was a step that earned Temujin greater loyalty to his entire population. He stated that everyone will be looked after particularly those who were forced to bear losses of soldier on the battlefield, on his own side, or another.

Change is, of course, slow. There were some who didn't want to adhere to the new rules to be patient and plunder the riches. Temujin quickly demonstrated that he would not to allow his rules to be violated. The people who looted instead of putting an end to the enemies were stripped of their belongings. This was not the way of the aristocratic and there was a certain defiance towards Jamuqa.

It would create a gap between the aristocrats and ordinary people even further than it had been. But, his method of thinking made sure that the directly backed him was from Temujin. This helped to build their confidence in his power and strength.

The second battle in the battle against Tatars was a total victory. He conquered his Tatar people and took the control of their land. He killed all the leaders , and took the rest of them into his clan. He employed adoption and marriage to integrate clans from other clans to his. It was an extremely effective method.

Temujin was aware that killing chiefs of the tribes that were not his was not going to make everyone happy. But, he also proved that intermarriage and the birth of a son to the mother of his choice was an effective way of embracing the Tatar and ease the anger of some. It was successful.

Don't Leave No One Behind

A commitment to loyalty within the army is essential to ensure that soldiers are safe from the combatants. "Brother's in arms" is a well-known concept in the present, however Temujin was the very first warrior and leader to begin the tradition in his own unique way. The idea of adoption and intermarrying wasn't enough (Weatherford (2004)). He required a method to make sure that everyone could be tolerant of each other and not fight over who was the best.

The next step to gain the trust of a fierce, loyal group of people was to reform his army. The year 1203, the Temujin directed an overhaul in his troops. He organized his troops into a "squad" composed of 10. They were all siblings to one another regardless of their place of background or kinship. They were required to fight for and live as brothers. Ten of the 10 squads formed the zagun comprising 100 men. Temujin created one of 100 zaguns into a battalion. It was an Mingan of 11,000 warriors. The Mingan joined to create the Tumen which was the 10000 warriors.

Temujin always chose to be the Tumen leader. Tumen. He needed a faithful person to take on this position, and as well as one who had the ability to ensure that the Tumen could be successful in their victory. Family members, like brothers, fathers, and sons were divided into groups of different kinds, but allowed to train together. In the field, he would prefer to split the lineages to ensure the loyalty of all. At the time, Temujin had about 95 Mingans which is roughly 80,000 soldiers. It isn't clear how many however, it is definitely within the range of.

At the point of this, Temujin began calling his followers "the The People from the Felt Walls," to signify that he had joined with the Tatars as well as the Mongols (Weatherford 2004).

Ong Khan as well as Ong Khan and Fight of the Khans

Ong Khan kept Jamuqa along with Temujin under his wing. They were still pitted against one another. However, it was evident the fact that Ong Khan was closing in to the point of his death. It was now time in the midst of 20 years trying to unify the Mongols and the Mongols, for Temujin to demand that Ong Khan to choose a clear successor, a clear decision in favor of one or the other.

Temujin asked for a marriage to Jochi his eldest son of his children, and Ong Khan's sister. Should the proposal be approved the wedding would be accepted. Ong Khan was in favor of Temujin. Ong Khan refused. He wanted his son to be the leader, but Ong Khan was not a talented person and had no followers that was his own within Ong Khan's followers.

The Kereyid believed that Temujin was inferior. Ong Khan's family still adhered to the aristocratic views. Initially, Ong Khan refused the marriage however the force Genghis Khan held was terrifying. Ong Khan decided to set up the stage for Temujin. Ong Khan accepted

Temujin's marriage and then plotted to kill Temujin as his father was killed.

Temujin had left the majority of his troops in the dust. There were not enough soldiers with him to fight and stand at the top of the stairs. He ordered his entire group to leave in different directions, and he risked the entire of what he'd gained. Raid after raid swarmed him as he attempted to defend his family. Temujin did not just have to acknowledge his heritage and believe that nothing has changed, but also was also confronted with his own internal struggle.

How can a man overcome the biggest hurdle he faces, defeat of his ambitions and goals when confronted with an aristocratic lineage?

It's an issue that will be addressed in the near future. As a result of the raids and the new fighting, some soldiers quit Khan returning on Ong Khan or Jemuqa. But, the 19 people together with him remained. They came from various families, with just one relative from Khan's family among the group. In the midst of their struggles, they killed horses and taking it as a symbol victory over their circumstances and survival, they were able to survive with only a few supplies.

Temujin did not quit. Whatever had occurred, regardless of the outcome, he had faith in himself and his faithful supporters. It is probable that he was determined to prove that his lineage doesn't matter. In the end, what is important is the desire to be successful.

There was a rumor of a banquet being hosted in the presence of Ong Khan to celebrate his triumph of bringing Temujin's remains from the steppes. This was the chance Temujin was seeking. He sent out his troops. It is likely that the story of his included a story that claimed a horse arose from heaven to protect him and his followers. He could have relied on the myth to demonstrate how he had been the preferred one to unify the entire nation of Mongolia.

His army was still in place despite his absence and rumored ruin. The army was aware about the legend and his strength. In a text message the army was instructed to go to the banquet in order to see Temujin.

Making the Hard Way

Temujin was not one to be able to travel in a manner in a place where his presence was immediately recognized. He took his men along with him on what was called the "Lightning Advance" and walked into the steppes, and then the feast in a treacherous terrain that was not protected.

What would make an enemy defend in a place that didn't make sense? This is exactly what Temujin believed. They couldn't. The difficult, remote path allowed Temujin to arrive sooner than anyone anticipated. Temujin arrived, along with his troops, encircling his Kereyid camp. For three days, they battled, the Kereyid fighting to retreat from the advance of the army. Ong Khan's left-wingers made their way to Temujin. The president accepted them, so it was not risk of harm or treachery for Ong Khan.

The threat of a coup against their former leader could lead to inflicting treachery on him. The majority of the army of Ong Khan was taken over by Temujin's hordes and not by the end, but rather by the way of allowing their members to become part of. Ong Khan as well as his army fled in different directions. Then Ong Khan's son fled the city to seek refuge in south. Contrary to Temujin the latter was unable to make it through. He was stricken by water deprivation while in desert.

Jamuqa was forced to run away. His followers began to abandon him , in spite that of supernatural security Genghis Khan appeared to possess and the capacity to endure the challenges.

Jamuqa migrated to his home tribe of the Naiman tribe. The Naiman's were one of the main tribes of Mongolia who ruled Mongolia. They were the only clan that Temujin did not attempt to take on. Ong Khan was also trying to reach the Naiman.

The effort to defeat and capture his foes failed however, rather than let his followers view that as a failure Temujin was determined to bring down the reputation that was Ong Khan.

Ong Khan's death

Genghis Khan might not have had the victory in the sense of killing Ong Khan and his son however they both died for their ejection of Temujin. Ong Khan was on his own when he landed on the border of the Naiman Confederacy. It was awe-inspiring that the elderly man, on his own, without an emissary could be such a formidable warrior. The guard was convinced that the man must be insane or was trying to fool the Naiman guard the guard shot him dead.

Chapter 9: The Naiman Confederacy

The legends spread about the deaths of Ong Khan and Naiman chief Tayang Khan. The story was that the head of Ong Khan was removed and placed on an altar made of a costly white fabric. This would have been far from the Mongols and not an act of honor , as the wife of Tayang allegedly intended it to be. Tayang continued to commit atrocities by beating his head when it was discovered within the room.

It was not about the manner in which Ong Khan had been treated however, how Genghis Khan utilized the incident to benefit himself. The Naiman's were aiding Jamuqa as well as being an extremely strong tribe, which was a part of Genghis Khan's path to total unity.

The battle could have begun at the front, however, Genghis used the story of Ong Khan to denigrate Tayang. Genghis informed the Mongols that Tayang had no respect in his circle of relatives, which included the wife he had no respect for. He claimed that Tayang was just an instrument for his wife. Also, it was said that she was not a fan for the

Mongols and believed that they were just savages.

As the news spread, the Mongols became angry. They began to worship Temujin, their commander. The Naiman's attempted to counter this by taking on the Mongol and showing how weak their Mongols were. Temujin exploited the Naiman's behaviour to gain his own advantage.

In the evening, he set off five campfires in the hills in their camp. The tiny force Temujin carried with him appeared to be much bigger than what it actually was. The tensions continued to increase in the period between 1202 and 1204, till 1204, when the Year of the Rat (1204) represented the final battle of the two sides: Temujin along with the Naimans as well as Jamuqa.

Genghis Khan demonstrated his leadership skills by:

* Starting small, unpredictable skirmishes.

* Temujin advanced by a small Moving Bush or Tumbleweed formation of men.

The commander disperse his troops in order to put them around the camp making sure they moved at dawn, allowing them to prepare for ambush.

* Naimans was unable to determine the number of people attacking, or how many people were being protected on all sides.

* The squads of Temujin's dispersed in different locations, making it difficult to follow them all.

* Genghis Khan employed an Lake Formation that required Naiman warriors to disperse and thin for attack.

The third strategy Temujin employed, was to group into the Chisel Formation that was a slender formation however, it was extremely deep.

The battle did not end with a huge battle but the warriors were scattered. At night, several of the Naiman left. Genghis Khan didn't let his troops follow. Instead, they stood resilient in the face of Tayang as well as Jamuqa. With just a few left fighting, Tayang fell. Tayang's death marked that the end of Naiman Confederacy. Jamuqa went missing into the forests.

In the future at 42 old, Jamuqa has to live as an outcast. Jamuqa was part of a bandit group and ate wild animals. Karma seems to have provided Jamuqa precisely the same thing that Genghis was forced to endure in his childhood. Nothing more than the things he was able to get to live on.

1205 Jamuqa had been captured in 1205, by some of his followers. They took the captive to Temujin to offer him a token for the ending of the reign of Jamuqa. As Temujin was loyal and loyalty, he didn't pay the soldiers who brought the blood-brother, who was captured, and the enemies to his house. They were executed before Jamuqa because of their unfaithfulness to Jamuqa.

Jamuqa after a lengthy confession said he'd like to be a better friend after death than he was in his death. Temujin was able to forgive Jamuqa as he asked them to become brothers once more.

Temujin was on the verge of bringing the entire Mongols under his reign. He had provided an alternative way of living that saw the aristocrats killed for their shadiness. He was furious over every injustice that was dealt to him, including the Taichyiud for murdering his father and making him a slave as well as the Merkits for abducting his wife. Over the course of those twenty plus years, he retaliated and demanded loyalty and he got it.

It is possible that he was portrayed as a bloodthirsty criminal However, when one looks at his actions, and the actions of his enemies He rose from the ashes and showed the importance of integrity and fairness were. The man who claimed to call himself the most powerful of the chiefs he made sure that Temujin would be able to take the title, and his supporters happily granted it to Temujin.

A year later, the Khuriltai conferred on his title chief among chiefs. He was the new head of Mongolia but this wasn't enough for this hero/villain. There was more to conquer: there was the entire world.

Chapter 10: Re Conquering The World-

Western Xia

Genghis Khan launched small attacks in Western Xia. Genghis Khan would carry on these raids until 1207 and then in 1209, he began an invasion of massive proportions into Xia as well as China. This war wasn't easy. Xia was a strong military force and an advantageous position on the land to fend off the bulk of the assaults. However there was a diverted river close to Yinchuan and led to the surrender of the Emperor Li Anquan in 1210.

The river actually killed the majority of Genghis Khan's soldiers, but Genghis Khan's men were powerful, and Jin, the ruler Jin was unwilling to help Western Xia. Instead, the ruler of Jin would like the two sides weaker in order to be able to sneak into Yinchuan and take it. Genghis Khan was armed with more power than was currently close to Yinchuan. They were also trying to figure ways to break through the city's walls and attempting to discover the weaknesses. The water had destroyed every crop Western Xia depended on. There was simply no better choice than to let Genghis Khan to win.

Western Xia was currently Genghis Khan's, however this didn't necessarily mean that war was over. The Jurched were, despite being generally defeated, had the Golden Khan in China. An envoy was assigned to talk with Genghis concerning subjugation on behalf of his brother, the former Jurched ruler. Genghis had reached his mid-forties at the time and was not willing to bow to anyone. Genghis didn't have to.

There was a nation, and perhaps more than 100,000 soldiers within his armies. Western Xia decided to become the vassal to Mongolia as well as Genghis Khan. They joined forces to bring conflict to Jin and Genghis Khan, which lasted up to 23 years.

However, this wasn't the only conflict Genghis Khan was engaged in. The Xia might have been defeated by Genghis Khan however, there were other nations. The Jurched or inhabitants who lived in Western Xia, saw many nations falling within them. This is one reason why the current ruler needed to concede. Genghis Khan was already the Tangut who had more knowledge about battle in cities than on steppes.

Genghis Khan was forced to come up with alternative methods because the Khan was unsure of how to conquer city walls. This is why he attempted to divert water which was successful, but eventually, he had to remove his own camp.

The Gobi Crossing

The journey to China required crossing The Gobi Desert. This happened prior to fighting with Xia. The desert was large and was not easy to traverse. It was nothing more than sand. Genghis Khan had to go on the journey with all the equipment he'd need to live and fight. The army was armed equipped with all the resources required, including food, water and an entire supply chain that was quite difficult to navigate. This was not something that most people would have thought of doing or even attempted.

But, Genghis Khan had ambitions and he aimed to make the dream come true. That's what it appeared to be. What is the point of trying to cross the vast desert and venture beyond the boundaries of China when there was nothing to gain. Of of course trading with China was a possibility that would provide a great benefit to the Mongolians.

Evidently, Genghis Khan was aware of the importance of trade in the previous years and realized that wealth and knowledge could generate a wealth that was enough to establish a nation economically and politically.

It is believed that Genghis Khan achieved so much success, eventually uniting Mongolia in his reign, that the Khan wanted to extend his capabilities further, while also making sure that his empire was capable of surviving.

He was aware that his life would not last long. It was just an issue of time before the time came for him to die as the Mongols did not have the longevity that humans do. As a legacy of his legacy as the Mongol Empire, it would be logical for him to think of different ways to ensure that his Mongol Empire reigned for centuries.

China does not want an empire that was so powerful on their borders, and there was fighting and raids to prevent Genghis Khan from growing in power. Whatever his motives and motives, which we can't be certain about but it is well known that within just 17 years, the Khan consolidated the expansion into

China and around the world. This was the push that his family would undertake.

Genghis Khan's strategic military plan was implemented and was highly efficient in the desert as well as his homeland. The process of traversing the desert, exploring every terrain and way to travel was an integral element of his military strategy. He wanted to ensure that he was aware of where he could go , without jeopardizing his plans. Scouts were sent out in different directions to figure out where and how to escape should he need to. This was also a means to figure out the best method to enter China as well as the other countries where he could eventually transfer his legacy to.

It was noted in historical books that the Genghis Khan's troops were able to travel thousands of miles, but without having a lot of food or water. They were able to survive in the conditions that Chinese would have to die in.

It was the culmination of their grit and his tactics ensured that he was able to survive when he was defeated. The traditional armies would go on a specific way, a route that was marked and secure. The soldiers would proceed to their next final destination. But Khan's army wasn't as organized. They were spread out. There was always a group of troops in the vicinity, to guard their flanks and sides, as well as their front and ensure that no enemies could be able to enter through a route which was not secured.

It was the movements of his troops and his determination to traverse through the Gobi Desert that worried Xia. This is also the reason why they decided to surrender. They were aware that Genghis Khan was not going to concede defeat. He would never stop trying and trying to win, and when reinforcements appeared at Xia it was almost a certain outcome that Xia would be defeated. The commander of Xia could have been aware of that and was aware that they would not endure with only a small amount of food.

Victory over Xia was only the beginning. He needed to take on Jin to bring down the Song Dynasty and take control over China.

The order of events followed:

"In 1219 Genghis Khan fought his first ever real war against Jin. Jin.

* He was the first to join Khwarezmian Dynasty. Khwarezmian Dynasty.

Khwarezmian Dynasty

The dynasty was situated within central China. From 1219 to 1227 Genghis Khan was working to expand his empire around the dynasty, as being in direct combat in his Khwarezmian army. Genghis Khan sent his troops out in the Islamic states to expand his empire more to India, Western Europe, and Arabia.

Genghis Khan didn't intend to keep fighting his foes in new nations. However, this does not mean that they didn't know that he was genuinely willing to pledge allegiance to new nations and maintain the peace he pledged to keep.

From the outside the outside, it would be more frightened to think that Genghis Khan might in some way change alliances. In all likelihood, he repeatedly switched alliances with Mongol leaders in the hopes to conquer Mongolia and also paying back those who had betrayed Genghis Khan in kind.

China was apprehensive about an expanding empire, just and so did its Khwarezmian

Dynasty. In the beginning, Genghis Khan approached the dynasty, asking to become a neighbor and to trade with them in peace. Shah Muhammad was not willing to sign a peace agreement however, he signed it. It was not long after the peace agreement was signed that a Mongol caravan carrying envoys to Otrar, Khwarezmian was decimated.

It was considered to be an act of aggression and an unambiguous appeal to the arms. Genghis Khan was a shrewd commander with a wealth of intelligence sources in the period and spies who traveled across the Silk Road. Through collecting data, Genghis Khan was able to build an army that had an organization that was different from the previous conflicts. Genghis Khan was sure to increase his cavalry, who were already in high demand. The siege wars he was taught by the Chinese because of his relationship with Xia.

He had been taught about gunspowder and siege bows along with battering rams. Bows could shoot arrows up to 20 feet. Through the combination of this capability and the network of intelligence, Genghis Khan amassed so vast knowledge that he could know the economic, military and political situation of all adversaries and the present countries bordering Mongolia.

Genghis Khan also grew his army to around the 400,000- 700,000 figure. It is not possible to be certain of the number of people who were part of his army since they were in different countries , and thus were spread across the globe. This also enabled him to win battles that he fought.

It took only 2 years Genghis Khan to acquire enough information about the Khwarezmian to eliminate their family dynasty. As with many battles, Genghis Khan was able kill the leaders, engulf the ordinary people, and expand his market for trade even more.

Chapter 11: Jin And His Legacy

The Mongol- Jin War was ongoing during 23 years. Genghis Khan did not believe it was necessary to be second only to China. Genghis Khan also was not in agreement with the sending of honors and tributes in Mongolia to China like they had done previously. China was definitely a powerful country, forged numerous dynasties and winning numerous battles. But Jin's population of 20million and his 700,000-strong army wasn't going to suffice to keep Genghis Khan's military skills. Genghis Khan was focused on trade and took over his share of the Silk Road trades.

He was open to setting an agreement with the Jin in the event that they considered him to be an equal partner and did not attempt to force his people in slavery. After the war was completed and the peace treaty ratified and the peace treaty dissolved, it's no wonder that Genghis Khan was not keen to join an unending war or consider any treaty which would favor him.

It was also known that Jin was known for kidnapping people, stealing their money and then slaughtering them. If Genghis Khan appeared weak, then his nation and his empire would be put at risk. But he was aware that Jin was extremely rich. There was many silver dollars for him to gather and use to pay his army.

Genghis Khan also discovered an advantage , when Genghis Khan sent spies into Jin camp. Jin camp. The Jin were fighting. There was a war within the Jin. Insofar as Genghis Khan profited from internal conflicts that were constantly developing, he was able to be victorious.

Kyzsl Kum Desert Kyzsl Kum Desert

Khan was adamant about the present-day Uzbekistan. It was a major city in The Jin Dynasty. He was keen to be shrewd regarding how he approached the city instead of going on the standard roads, the man took a different route. In the past, Kyzsl Kum Desert was considered unhospitable. It was a place where people could go to die, rather than and take on the gate of city. This didn't matter to Genghis Khan, because his spies and scouts gave the possibility of getting through the desert and not die.

When Jin arrived with his army of great strength there was fear as the most prominent emotion. According to historians, 20,000 Jin warriors flew away from the city and left the city open for Mongols to capture. The capture of Bukhara was a loss in itself. This also led to city sackings, and each one of the cities run by Jin Samarkand was next attacked. Whatever weaknesses Genghis Khan could discover was exploited by Genghis Khan.

His victory over the entirety of China wasn't to last. He could never comprehend how his work was rewarded and allowed the Mongol Empire would eventually rule the entirety of China and portions from India, Europe, and Russia.

His Demise and Legacy

Each of these actions, including the one that was finally won by the Jin caused Genghis Khan's legacy. In spite of all the attacks against China's dynasties it was not until the death of Genghis Khan in 1227 to achieve the victory to be complete.

Xia must be completely destroyed in terms of any attack. The entire empire had to be brought down to knees. The best way to make the whole of China collapse into its own puddle was for it to go to Yinchuan.

There are many myths which tell of Genghis Khan's demise. One story states that Genghis Khan was wounded in an incident in the month of August 1227. This caused an infection and death. The injury may be the result of the fall of his horse or by an injury from an arrow to his leg. There is another less likely hypothesis that some historians and researchers think. They believe that he was ageing and reached the point of no return and passed away peacefully with his family in his arms.

Genghis Khan had the ability support his family by winning battles. Genghis Khan was able to hand over his sons to manage different areas of land that were claimed and then choose a successor to run his Mongol Empire. The Mongol Empire would not last. It was just 100 years later, all of Genghis Khan's works were divided. Mongolia became a smaller state again as China was taken back under the current Chinese dynasty. Russia was able to fight back and took back their territory.

It is apparent that with no supreme Mongolian leader, the Mongol Empire would not be able to keep its huge expanse. Maybe his great and grand grandson were not as able to meet the demands of the empire, or perhaps the changes in technology which made it difficult.

Despite the demise of the empire, Genghis Khan left an impression across the globe. Genghis Khan left his military strategy, intelligence, as well as his knowledge of trade. He also spread the idea. He promoted fairness in the world that did not have it. Unfortunately, his fairness of his ideas has not been a success however, some of his ideas have.

Chapter 12: Genghis' Various Sexual Relationships With Kids

In the same way as was typical for successful Mongol men, Genghis Khan had many courtesans and partners. He usually took wives as well as courtesans from empires and the societies he controlled, they were often princesses or queens that were captured or presented to Genghis Khan. Genghis Khan provided many of his high-status companions their own personal ordos or camps to live in and to manage. The camps also had minor spouses and courtesans and even children. It was the responsibility of Kheshig (Mongol royal guard) to protect the yurts that were the homes of Genghis Khan's associates. Guards had to be attentive to the particular yurt or camp where Genghis Khan slept. The yurts could change at night, as he checked out various partners. When Genghis Khan went off to conquer his enemies He usually carried one of his partners with him and left his other partners (and his courtesans) to oversee the empire in his absence. Perhaps that's one method to manage your life.

Borte

The wedding ceremony that took place between Borte and Genghis Khan (then named Temujin) was planned by her father and Yesugei the father of Temujin at the age of at the age of ten, and he was nine years old. Temujin remained in her home with the rest of her family until when he was called to care for his mom and other younger siblings, as a result from the poisonings of Yesugei from Tatar wanderers. Then, in 1178, around seven years on, Temujin went down the Keluren River to find Borte. The father of Borte's noticed that Temujin had come back to marry Borte and had the set "joined as man and wife". With the permission of her father Temujin moved Borte along with her mother to stay in his yurt, which was the family's. Borte's wedding dowry was a beautiful dark sable black coat. After the wedding between them three Merkits stormed their family camp in the early morning and took Borte. The girl was handed over by one of the warriors they killed as a reward of the war. Temujin was extremely upset by the abduction of his spouse and remarked to his wife that "bed was empty" and that his "breast was broken". Temujin was able to save her several months later, with the assistance of his friends Wang Khan and Jamukha. The majority of scholars define this incident as one of key crossing points in the life of Temujin that led him on the path to becoming an emperor.

"As the ransacking and pillaging continued, Temujin walked between the crowds who were leaving fast, shouting"Borte! Borte! He then was able to spot her, as Woman Borte was amongst those fleeing people. She was able to hear the voice of Temujin and, recognizing that she heard it, she left the cart and ran towards him. As it was still dark the two girls each acknowledged Temujin's reins as well as tether. They both grabbed them. The moonlight was shining as he surveyed them and greeted Woman Borte, and they immediately fell into one another's arms." The Secret History of the Mongols

Borte was held for eight months before being brought back to Jochi shortly after her rescue. This left a question mark as to who the father of the child was as her captor was able to use her as an "marriage companion" and possibly fertilized her. However Temujin allowed Jochi remain in the family and treated that he was his child. Borte had three sons: Chagatai (from 1183 to 1242), Ogedei (from 1186 until 1241) And Tolui (from 1191 until about 1232). Temujin also had a lot of children who were married to other people However, they were not included from the succession. However, only Borte's sons can be said as his beneficiaries. Borte was also mother to several daughter, Kua Ujin Bekhi, Alakhai Bekhi, Alaltun, Tumelun, Checheikhen and Tolai. However, the shaky survival of Mongol records makes it unclear if she brought into her life each of them.

Yesugen

In the course of his war to fight the Tatars, Temujin fell for Yesugen and accepted her as a female partner. It was her daughter who was an Tatar leader known as Yeke Cheren, whom Temujin's army had killed during the time of battle. After the battle to defeat the Tatars was finished, Yesugen, one of the survivors, went to Temujin who was sleeping with her. In the Secret History of the Mongols when they were in the process of in love, Yesugen demanded Temujin to take care of her with respect and not abandon her. If Temujin was seen to be in agreement in this regard, Yesugen advised that he also married his sister Yesui.

He is loved by him. Yisugen Qatun stated, 'If it is pleasing to the Qa'an I will be looked after by him and consider me an individual and a person worthy of keeping. My older sister, known as Yisui is a different person to me. She's definitely fit as the position of a ruler.'

- the Hidden History of The Mongols

Both Tatar siblings, Yesugen and Yesui, were subsequently part of Temujin's main partners, and they were given their own camps that they managed. Temujin also claimed a third female from the Tatars and a courtesan who is not identified.

Yesui

Based on the advice by her younger Sister Yesugen, Temujin had his men find and kidnap Yesui. When she was handed to Temujin's attention, he saw her just as sweet as he had promised, and she was married to him. The other partners, mothers sisters and daughters of the Tatars were slashed and handed over the Mongol guys. Tatar sisters Yesugen and Tatar Sisters, Yesugen and Yesui, were among Genghis Khan's most famous wives. Genghis Khan brought Yesui along as he embarked on his final expedition to fight Tangut. Tangut empire.

Khulan

Khulan was a part of Mongol history when her father who was Merkit chief Dayir Usan, gave up to Temujin during the winter of 1203-2004 in 1203 and handed her over to Temujin. But, at minimum, according to the Secret History of the Mongols, Khulan and her dad were snatched by Naya'a the Temujin's officer who clearly was trying to shield the two from Mongol fighters who were a neighbor to. After arriving three days late than they had was expected, Temujin believed Naya'a's motive was his sexual desires to Khulan to aid her father and her. When Temujin was questioning Naya's, Khulan spoke out in his defense and urged Temujin's desire to be with her and to examine her virginity in person that he was happy with.

In the end, Temujin agreed to Dayir Usan's resignation as well as Khulan as his new wife. However, Dayir Usan later withdrew his surrender, however, the rest of his subjects were ultimately beaten down as well as his belongings taken away and he was himself executed. Temujin continued to carry out military initiatives against the Merkits until their final dispersal in 1218. Khulan was able to achieve a high recognition as a Temujin's partner and was in charge of one of the biggest wives' camps where other wives, courtesans and other children, and even animals were a part of the camp. She introduced to the world the boy named

Gelejian who later went on to join Borte's sons and their dad's army work.

Moge Khatun

Moge Khatun was lady courtesan to Genghis Khan, and eventually became the wife of Genghis Khan's daughter Ogedei Khan. The Persian historian Ata-Malik Juvayni records that Moge Khatun "was handed the name of Chinggis Khan by a chief of the Bakrin people and he loved her a lot." Ogedei loved her too, and she was a companion when he was on the hunt for. She's not listed as having any children and, in the past, this wasn't the most pleasant situation for women. Children were generally viewed as a plus and were one of the main reasons for women to live in those times. Professions were not as prevalent as they are now.

Juerbiesu

Juerbiesu is an Empress from the Qara Khitai, Mongol Empire, and Naiman. She was popularly attractive in the plains. Her first position was as a courtesan of Inanch Bilge Khan and following his death, she was the accompanist of his son Tayang Khan. In view of the fact that Tayang Khan was an ineffective leader, Juerbiesu was in control of almost all authority in Naiman political life.

She had a daughter named princess Hunh and Yelu Zhilugu, the ruler of Liao. Following the time that Genghis Khan caused damage to his people Naiman population in the Naiman region and Tayang Khan's life was lost, the Juerbiesu had made offensive remarks about Mongols and their clothes, describing their appearances as filthy and smelly. In the end she changed her assertions as she went over to Genghis Khan's tent in the camp. He asked her about the remarks but was immediately attracted by her attractiveness. After a night spent in his company, she vowed to do his best and was accepted as his empress. The status she was given to her only second that of Khulan as well as Borte.

Ibaqa Beki

Ibaqa was the oldest child of Kerait head Jakha Gambhu. He teamed up together with Genghis Khan to defeat the Naimans during the year 1204. In the course of this partnership, Ibaqa was given to Genghis Khan to be the female spouse. She was the mother of Begtutmish, who was married to Genghis Khan's son Jochi and Sorghaghtani Begki and

Tolui, who were married to Genghis Khan's child Tolui . After approximately two years of no children in the union, Genghis Khan suddenly separated Ibaqa and gave her to general Jurchedei as who was a member of the Uru'ut clan who killed Jakha Gambhu when the latter changed sides against Genghis Khan. The reason for the marriage is not known in the book The Secret History of the Mongols, Genghis Khan gave Ibaqa to Jurchedei in exchange for his role in the injury to Nilga Senggum in 1203 and later in the killing of Jakha Gambhu. In another way, Rashid al-Din in Jami' al-tawarikh states that Genghis Khan split Ibaqa because of a horrific nightmare that God ordered him to give her away immediately and Jurchedei happened be guarding the tent of the camp. In spite of this, Genghis Khan enabled Ibaqa to retain her title of Khatun when she remarried and requested to be left an oath from her dowry so that it could keep her in mind. According to the sources, Ibaqa was quite rich.

Chapter 13: The Way He Unified Mongolian Federations

In the 12th century's early years In the early 12th century, the Main Asian plateau north of China was divided into several popular tribal confederations. These included Naimans Merkits, Tatars, Khamag Mongols, and Keraites who were usually adversaries as evident by random raids, revenge attacks and ransacking.

First attempts at power

Temujin began his rise to power by pledging himself as an all-weather ally (or according to some sources as a vassal) to his father's anda (sworn brother or blood brother) Toghrul, who was Khan of the Keraites He was also recognized by the Chinese name "Wang Khan" that is what the Jurchen Jin dynasty gave him in 1197. This friendship was strengthened after Borte was snatched in the hands of Merkits. Temujin contacted Toghrul for help and Toghrul offered to give 20,000 in his Keraite warriors and suggested Temujin be accompanied by his young close friend

Jamukha who was to end up as the The Khan for his personal tribe The Jadaran.

While the project did save Borte and utterly outclassed the Merkits paved to the breakup in Temujin as well as Jamukha. Before that they were blood brothers (anda) and pledging to remain always dedicated.

Rift together with Jamukha as well as beat Dalan Balzhut

When Jamukha and Temujin drifted away from their relationships, they both began pairing up, and they became rivals. Jamukha favored the conventional Mongolian elite, whereas Temujin utilized a meritocratic approach that attracted more diverse and lower-class of followers. In the wake of his earlier defeat against the Merkits and a declaration from the Shaman Kokochu of Temujin was the Eternal Blue Sky had set aside the entire world for Temujin's rise, Temujin was able to ascend to power in 1186. Temujin was selected as the as the khan of the Mongols. Infuriated by this rising power, Jamukha assaulted Temujin in the year 1187 , with an army of around 30000 men. Temujin brought his followers together to fight the assault, but was ruthlessly defeated during the Fight of Dalan Balzhut. But, Jamukha was terrified and drove away any prospective followers after boiling up 70 male slaves in boiling cauldrons. Toghrul was Temujin's client and was exiled to Qara Khitai. The existence of Temujin's client for the next ten years remains not certain, as the historical records are mostly silent on the time.

Return to the power.

In 1197 In 1197, the Jin launched an attack on their official vassal, Tatars along with The Keraites as well as the Mongols. Temujin led a portion of the assault, and, after a successful his and Toghrul were returned to the Jin to the positions of authority. The Jin conferred Toghrul with the prestigious the title Ong Khan and Temujin with the lower title,"j'aut quri.

In the year 1200, the main adversaries in the Mongol confederation (typically the "Mongols") were the Naimans in the west and to the west, Merkits in the northern region and to the north, Tanguts towards the southern and the Jin to the east.

In his reign and victory over rivals Temujin departed from Mongol tradition in many important ways. He transferred authority to those who benefitted and remained committed rather than the ties to family. In exchange for his absolute conformity and adhering to following the Yassa legal code, Temujin offered his fighters and people a share of the future battle spoils. If he was able to beat rivals and defeated them, he did not rebuke their warriors or abandon their people. Instead, he brought the oppressed people to his side and integrated its members into his own group of people. He even had his mother adopt orphans from the dominant people, and then bring the children into his own family. These political changes influenced a great determination amongst the people who were defeated and made Temujin stronger every time he achieved success.

Rift in conjunction with Toghrul

Senggum was the son of Toghrul (Wang Khan) He was in awe of Genghis Khan's power growing and connection to his father. He was believed to be preparing to murder Genghis Khan. Although Toghrul was said to have been slayed on several times from Genghis Khan, Toghrul reacted to his son and ended up not cooperating to Genghis Khan. Genghis Khan was aware of Senggum's intentions and eventually beat Toghrul as well as his fellow patriots.

One of the rifts that occurred later among Genghis Khan and Toghrul was the refusal of Toghrul to offer his daughter an engagement with Jochi, Genghis Khan's first child. It was unprofessional in Mongolian culture and led to an outbreak of conflict. Toghrul joined forces with Jamukha and was already in opposition to Genghis Khan's troops. However the conflict among Toghrul and Jamukha and the defection of their allies from Genghis Khan, led to Toghrul's defeat. Jamukha was absent throughout the conflict. This loss was the reason to the demise and destruction of the Keraite people.

After having dominated his way across all of the Alchi Tatars, Keraites, and Uhaz Merkits, and obtaining at least one spouse every time, Temujin shifted to the next danger on the steppes that is the Turkic Naimans, under the leadership under the direction of Tayang Khan with whom Jamukha and his followers sought refuge. The Naimans were not going to quit, even though a number of sectors once again voted in favor of Genghis Khan.

In the year 1201 the khuruldai chose Jamukha to be Gur Khan, "universal ruler" the title that was used for the rulers in the Qara Khitai. Jamukha's assumption of this title was his final violation with Genghis Khan and Jamukha created a group of his opponents. In the midst of the dispute, several generals departed from Jamukha. this includes Subutai Jelme, who was Jelme's most popular younger brother. After some fighting, Jamukha was committed Genghis Khan by his own troops in 1206.

As per the Secret History, Genghis Khan once again extended his friendship to Jamukha. Genghis Khan killed those who had were a sham to Jamukha by stating that he did not want unfaithful members of his army. Jamukha rejected the offer, stating that there is only only one star in heaven and he pleaded for a dignified death. The standard was to die in a manner that did not spill blood especially through a back injury. Jamukha favored this method of death, even though it was reported that he the generals of his adversaries to boil alive.

Only Ruler of the Mongol plains (1206)

The section from the Merkit clan that sided with that the Naimans had been defeated by Subutai who was an officer in Genghis Khan's personal security and later on became the one Genghis Khan's most successful leaders. The defeat of the Naimans led to Genghis Khan becoming the sole supreme ruler over the Mongol steppe. All populous confederations were destroyed or were unified under Genghis Khan's Mongol confederation.

The accounts of Genghis Khan's life are characterized by allegations of a number of deceit and sabotage. There were rifts with first allies, such as Jamukha (who also desired to be the ruler of the Mongol the Mongols) along with Wang Khan (his and his father's allies) and his son Jochi and his concerns with the most crucial shaman, who claimed to create a divide among him and his loyal brother Khasar. The tactics of his army showed a keen interest in studying the motivations of his rivals as demonstrated by his extensive surveillance network and Yam paths. He seemed to be an adept student, incorporating innovative ideas and innovations that found his way into, like Siege war from Chinese. He also was a shrewd person and demonstrated this by his method of using a linchpin to gauge against the linchpin which was used against those who were led by Jamukha.

So, by 1206 Genghis Khan was able to bring together or rule over the Merkits Naimans Mongols, Keraites, Tatars, Uyghurs, and other minorities under his control. This was an important job. It resulted in peace between the once warring population as well as a united army and political force. The union was later known as the Mongols. In a Khuruldai meeting made up of Mongol leaders, Genghis Khan was acknowledged as the Khan of the combined people, and was given the name "Genghis Khan". This title Khagan was given in his honor by his son as well as his inheritor Ogedei who claimed this title on behalf of himself (as Genghis Khan was to be declared posthumously to be the creator of the Yuan Dynasty).

In the Secret History of the Mongols the chieftains of the dominant people made a promise to Genghis Khan to declare:

"We will create you Khan and you will be riding in our midst, and fight our foes. We will throw ourselves like lightning onto your enemies. We'll bring you their most stunning females and girls, their lavish camping tents, as palaces."

Chapter 14: His Military Projects

It's difficult to summarize the many battles Genghis Khan fought for. Genghis Khan controlled a vast area of the world that was known to the world at the time. However, we'll endeavor to be a bit more thorough to make an effort in the next chapter.

Western Xia Dynasty

Through the political rise of Genghis Khan, Genghis Khan's Mongol Empire created by Genghis Khan and his allies shared western frontiers with Genghis Khan's allies of the Tangut Western Xia dynasty To the south and east of the Western Xia dynasty was the extremely militarily superior Jin Dynasty, founded by the Jurchens from Manchurian who controlled the northern part of China and were also the traditional rulers for their Mongolian people for many centuries.

Although it was less militarily superior to the adjacent Jin, Western Xia still put in an enormous influence on the nearby steppes in the north. After the loss of Keraites leaders Ong Khan to Temujin's emerging Mongol

Empire in 1203. Keriat chief Nilqa Senggum was the leader of a small group that he commanded into Western Xia before later being removed from the Western Xia terrain.

With his rival Nilga Senggum's temporary sanctuary located in Western Xia as a pretext for his attack, Temujin launched an offensive at the State in 1205 within the Edsin region. The following year, in 1206 Temujin became officially declared Genghis Khan, the ruler of all the Mongols which marked the primary beginning in the Mongol Empire, and the exact year in which the Emperor Huanzong of Western Xia was desposed by Li Anquan through an act of coup of etat. In 1207, Genghis conducted another raid on Western Xia, attacking the Ordos area , and then sacked Wuhai the main fort located along the Yellow River, before withdrawing in 1208. Genghis then began preparing for an invasion of a major scale and preparing his people as well as his army to get them ready for the war.

If he were to join Western Xia Temujin will gain a tribute-paying vassal and would also take over the management of the caravan routes through the Silk Roadway and supply the Mongols with substantial income. Furthermore to this, from Western Xia the Mongol leader could initiate raids against the richer Jin dynasty. He was firmly convinced that the younger and more efficient head of the Jin dynasty won't seek the aid of Western Xia. When the Tanguts requested assistance by the Jin dynasty but were not granted. Regardless of the initial difficulties with the recording of Western Xia cities, Genghis Khan was able to force the Emperor Renzong to accept the vassal status.

The Jin Dynasty

After the victory over Western Xia, Genghis Khan was ready to take on his Jin dynasty. Wanyan Jiujin who was the chief of the field of his Jin army, committed an oversight in his strategy of not attacking the Mongols in the first opportunity. Instead the Jin commander sent an messenger, Ming' an, to the Mongol side who defected, and informed the Mongols that they were in danger. Jin Army was on the other part of the pass. In the battle at Yehuling and Yehuling, the Mongols killed a number of Jin soldiers. in 1215 Genghis was able to take over the Jin capital city of Zhongdu (modern-day Beijing). As per Ivar

Lissner, the inhabitants were forced to shoot silver and gold cannons at the Mongols using their muzzle-loading guns as their metal supply to fire ammo ran out. The city was snatched and pillaged. The incident prompted the Jin ruler Emperor Xuanzong to relocate his capital to the south, to Kaifeng leaving the northern portion of his empire to Mongols. Between 1232-1233, Kaifeng fell down to the Mongols under the rule of Genghis's third child, Ogedei Khan. The Jin Dynasty fell in 1234 following the battle of Caizhou.

Qara Khitai

Kuchlug was the Khan deposed of the Naiman confederation which Temujin defeated and merged in the Mongol Empire, fled to the west and took over Khanate that was Qara Khitai (also referred to as the Western Liao since it was first built as the relics from the Liao dynasty). Genghis Khan chose to take over that Qara Khitai and thwart Kuchlug and possibly to take Kuchlug out of the power. In the meantime, Genghis Khan's Mongol army was exhausted after the 10 years of continuous commercialization within China in Kuchlug, who was a member of the Western

Xia as well as the Jin dynasties. This is why Genghis sent only the equivalent of 2 Tumen (20,000 army) against Kuchlug under his younger General, Jebe, referred to as "The Arrow".

With this little power that the Mongols were forced to alter their tactics and thereby trigger an internal conflict among Kuchlug's supporters which made Kuchlug's Qara Khitai more vulnerable to Mongol defeat. Then, Kuchlug's army was defeated by the west of Kashgar. Kuchlug was able to escape and was soon chased by Jebe's army, and was executed. In 1218, as a result from the loss of Qara Khitai, the Mongol Empire and its power reached as far west as Lake Balkhash, which surrounded Khwarazmia the Muslim state that extended to beyond the Caspian Sea to the west and the Persian Gulf and the Arabian Sea to the south.

Khwarazmian Empire

In the 13th century's early years in the 13th century, the Khwarazmian family was headed by Shah Ala ad-Din Muhammad. Genghis Khan recognized the potential benefits of Khwarazmia to be an industrial trade partner through its Silk Roadway, and he at first organized 500 men in a caravan to establish the main trade links between the Empire. Genghis Khan, his family members and his leaders were involved in the caravan and invested silver, gold, silk various kinds of textiles and other materials, as well as pelts, to trade with Muslim dealers of the Khwarazmian areas. But, Inalchuq, the ruler of Otrar, the ruler of the Khwarazmian town of Otrar attacked the caravan and claimed that the caravan contained spies and, as a result, was a plot against Khwarazmia. The situation ended up becoming more complex due to the fact that the ruler refused to pay for the vandalism of the caravans and to turn over the culprits. Genghis Khan sent another group of three Ambassadors (2 Mongols and a Muslim) to meet with the Shah himself, instead of Inalchuq, the ruler. Inalchuq. The Shah ordered all the men shaved, and the Muslim was executed and then returned his head with the two remaining ambassadors. In a state of anger, Genghis Khan prepared one of his most infamous intrusion plans by putting together around 100,000 soldiers (10 tumens) and his most skilled generals as well as some from his own sons. Genghis Khan resigned as a leader along with a many soldiers in China and designated his followers as his family and named Ogedei as his immediate successor, and then he went towards Khwarazmia.

The Mongol army led by Genghis Khan, his generals and his sons traversed his Tien Shan mountains by going into the region that was ruled by Khwarazmian Empire. Khwarazmian Empire. After assembling information from numerous sources, Genghis Khan meticulously prepared his troops, and they were divided into three groups. The son of Genghis Khan Jochi was the leader of his first division into the northeast region of Khwarazmia. The 2nd division, under Jebe was secretly marched towards the southeast of Khwarazmia to form, together with one division, the pincer assault on Samarkand. The 3rd division, under Genghis Khan as well as Tolui marched to northwest and attacked Khwarazmia in that direction.

The army of the Shah was divided through a variety of internal conflicts as well as the Shah's decision to split his army into small groups that were based on different cities. The result was a definite fragmentation in the Khwarazmia's battles, since it enabled the

Mongols who were exhausted after a long trek, to immediately begin beating small portions of the Khwarazmian forces , rather than facing a united defense. The Mongol army quickly seized Otrar as a town Otrar and relied on a unique strategy and tactics. Genghis Khan ordered the massive massacre of many of the residents, and shackled the rest of the people in a gruesome execution. Inalchuq by placing molten silver in his eyes and ears in retribution for his conduct.

Genghis Khan's next birthplace was Bukhara, the capital of Bukhara that was not terribly built up, having just one moat and a wall and the common castle of Khwarazmian cities. The city's leadership allowed the entrance to the Mongols but the system of Turkish protectors occupied the castle of Bukhara for an additional 12 days. The survivors of in the castle was executed. artisans and artisans were sent back to Mongolia and young men who did not fight were made into the Mongolian army, and the remainder part of the populace was taken to slavery. Following Bukhara's surrender Bukhara, Genghis Khan also did the extraordinary thing of personally entering the city. After that, the city's elites and aristocrats taken to the mosque where they were able to hear him, via interpreters, addressed them about their actions and said: "If you had not committed a grave sin, God wouldn't have sent the same punishment as me upon you."

Following the defeat of Bukhara The way was now clear to the Mongols to take down the capital city of Samarkand that had stronger strongholds and a larger fort compared to Bukhara. In order to conquer the city the Mongols engaged in a long and intense mental warfare, including the use of captured Khwarazmian prisoners as bodyguards. After a couple of days, a handful of soldiers who remained who were loyal followers of the Shah were able to remain within the castle. When the fortress was destroyed, Genghis executed all soldiers who took up arms against Genghis. In the words of the Persian historical scholar Ata-Malik Jivayni the citizens of Samarkand were later required to leave the city and then put together on a plain in front of the city. There they were executed, and pyramids with headless heads were raised in to show their triumph. In the same way, Juvayni wrote that in the city of Termez which was located in South in Samarkand, "all the people of all ages, male and female were exiled to the plain and then split according to their usual fashion, and later all shot dead".

Juvayni's account about mass murders at these locations isn't confirmed by archaeology of the present. Instead of killing local populations or destroying the local population, the Mongols were more likely to subjugate the dominant and then either sent them to Mongolia to perform routine laborers or to keep them to use in the military. However, the influence was still massive destruction of the population. The building of a "pyramid of heads that had been severed" was not in Samarkand but in Nishapur in Nishapur, the place where Genghis Khan's sons in-law Toquchar were killed with an arrow fired out of the city's walls following the city's citizens protested. The Khan later allowed his daughter who was widowed who was expecting in the moment, to decide what fate the town would take and then she ordered that all the inhabitants was to be executed. The Khan also said that every pet cat, dog and all other animals living within the city would be slaughtered, "so that no living thing could endure the killing of her husband". The execution was performed by the Khan's youngest son Tolui. According to widely circulated but not proven stories the heads that were severed were then stacked in separate stacks for men, women and children.

Near the end of the war for Samarkand The Shah left the city and did not surrendering. Genghis Khan therefore ordered two Generals of his, Subutai and Jebe, to take down the remnants that remained of the Khwarazmian Empire. He provided the army with 20,000 soldiers and two years for this. The Shah died under the mystical guise of an island located in the Caspian Sea that he had returned to with his faithful troops.

At the same time, the wealthy city of trade Urgench was under the control by Khwarazmian forces. The assault on Urgench proved to be the most difficult battle of the Mongol invasion. The city was only destroyed when the protectors put up an imposing defense that fought block by block. Mongolian losses were greater than normal, due to the difficult task of adapting Mongolian strategies to city fighting. In normal circumstances, craftsmen were sent back to Mongolia as were children and girls. were given to Mongol warriors to serve as servants, and the remaining people were massacred. It is said that the Persian academic Juvayni mentions that the 50,000 Mongol fighters were assigned the task of killing twenty-four Urgench residents per one which means the equivalent of 1.2 million were murdered. These numbers are thought to be to be implausible in terms of logistics by modern scientists however, the execution of Urgench was certainly one of the bloodiest events.

Georgia, Crimea, Kievan Rus and Volga Bulgaria

After the demise of the Khwarazmian Empire in 1220, Genghis Khan gathered his troops from Persia and Armenia to go back in his homeland of the Mongolian steppes. Based on the concept of Subutai his Mongol army was split into two armies. Genghis Khan led the first army in a rout across Afghanistan along with northern India towards Mongolia and a second 20.000 (2 tumen) group marched through Caucasus and on into Russia under the command of generals Jebe as well as Subutai. They advanced into Armenia as well as Azerbaijan. The Mongols defeated the state of Georgia and seized the Genoese trade-fortress Caffa located in Crimea and then remained in the vicinity of to the Black Sea. Returning to their home, the Subutai's troops defeated the allied forces from the Cuman-the - Kipchaks as well as the poorly co-operating of 80,000 Kievan Rus' soldiers led by Mstislav the Strong of Halych and Mstislav III of Kiev who set out for the purpose of stopping the Mongols and their actions in the region. Subutai sent emissaries for the Slavic princes demanding a different peace however, the emissaries were killed. In the Fight of Kalka River in 1223, the forces of Subutai defeated the larger Kievan army. They could have been defeated by the nearby Volga Bulgars during the Fight of Samara Bend. There is no historical record aside from a short account of the Arab historical historian Ibn al-Athir, writing in Mosul around 1,800 kilometers (1,100 miles) from the scene. Diverse secondary sources from the past-- Morgan, Chambers, Groussetmention it was the Mongols actually defeated Bulgars. Bulgars, Chambers even going further and stating that the Bulgars created stories to inform the (just recently smashed) Russians that they had defeated the Mongols and pushed them out of their land. They Russian princes then called for peace. Subutai accepted the request, however he was not in a mental state to forgive the princes. Not only did the Rus put up a strong fight as well, but Jebe-Subutai's partner with whom he been fighting for many years was killed right prior to his death in the Fight of Kalka River. Like the customs of Mongol society for nobles and aristocracy, nobility was killed, and Russian princes were killed with an unbloody death. Subutai had a huge wooden platform on which the prince ate his meals with his generals. Six Russian princes including but not only Mstislav III, the king of Kiev was thrown under this platform , and then were crushed to death.

The Mongols were able to gain from hostages of the lush green pastures near that Bulgar terrain, allowing the preparation for the conquering Hungary in addition to Europe. Genghis Khan was able to recall Subutai's return to Mongolia rapidly later. The famous cavalry expedition conducted by Subutai and Jebe who covered the entire Caspian Sea beating all armies during their journey, remains unsurpassed to this day and the news of Mongol achievements started to leak across other nations, especially in Europe. The two projects are generally classified as reconnaissance efforts that attempted to understand the cultural and political aspects of the area. The two departments split in 1225 and both went into Mongolia. The invasions brought Transoxiana as well as Persia to the current powerful empire , while destroying any resistance that came along. Later , under Genghis Khan's grandson Batu along with his successor, the Golden Crowd, the Mongols returned to rule Volga Bulgaria and Kievan Rus' in 1237. The project was completed at the time of 1240.

Western Xia and Jin Dynasty

The vassal emperor of Tanguts (Western Xia) had previously refused to take part in the Mongol conflict to defeat Khwarezmid Empire. Khwarezmid Empire. Western Xia along with the beat Jin dynasty forged a alliance to fight the Mongols and relied on the plan to fight the Khwarazmians to stop their Mongols from reacting effectively.

In 1226, immediately after his return in the direction of the west Genghis Khan began a revengeful attack on the Tanguts. Genghis Khan's army swiftly defeated Heisui, Ganzhou, and Suzhou (not Suzhou, which is not Suzhou located in Jiangsu province) and later in the fall, he seized the city of Xiliang-fu. A number of Tangut generals was able to challenge his fellow Mongols to a battle near Helan Mountains but was beat. On November 1, Genghis attacked Lingzhou, the Tangut city Lingzhou and crossed the Yellow River, beating the Tangut relief army. As per legends, it was at this point that Genghis Khan was believed to have seen the 5 stars that was erected in the sky, and interpreted the vision into a prediction of his victory.

In 1227 Genghis Khan's forces attacked and destroyed the Tangut capital city of Ning Hia and went on to advance, capturing Lintiao-fu, Xining province, Xindu-fu and Deshun provinces at a rapid pace during the early spring. In Deshun Ma Jianlong, Tangut General Ma Jianlong set up a solid resistance for a few days, and led the charge against the intruders in front of the city gates. Ma Jianlong later passed away due to injuries sustained by shooting arrows during the battle. Genghis Khan, following his victory over Deshun and then went into Liupanshan (Qingshui County in Gansu Province) to escape the gruelling summer time.

Conclusion

Thank you for buying this book!

Temujin and the later Genghis Khan was both a hero as well as an antagonist. He was one of those who rose from his ashes to take revenge on his adversaries, while making his home more welcoming to all who lived and swore loyalty to his. He made sure that the aristocracy wasn't in the throne, only those who had the necessary skills were in the positions.

After a review of his actions in 1206, he became the type of person who would take over other people's land because he was strong enough to be able to do it. His military strategies, intelligence and loyalty enabled him to create terror in other people and destroy certain nations without causing a huge amount of bloodshed.

Temujin's early years portray the image of a weakling and a man of no ambition. We'll never know the answer to whether he could have become the most powerful Khan of Mongolia and the world, but for the loss of his father and the hardships caused by it. It can be concluded that his perception of loyalty and fairness might not be the same if were he not remained at the side of his dad.

He would not have experienced the anger against his tribe, and those of the various clans in the event that clear succession and the oath of his father been established. The killing of his father may have affected his character and interests in the same way as the circumstances he was put in.

Maybe greed led him to conquer the world, rather than being content with Mongolia However, it was his history which made him strive for something bigger than just trying to live beyond 10 years old.

Thanks and best of luck!

www.ingramcontent.com/pod-product-compliance
Lightning Source LLC
Chambersburg PA
CBHW050403120526
44590CB00015B/1810